With the Compliments of

KOREA FOUNDATION **KF**

한국국제교류재단

Seocho P.O.BOX 227 Seoul, KOREA Tel:82-2-2151-6545, Fax:82-2-2151-6592

Ask a Korean Dude

Ask a Korean Dude

Written and Compiled by **Kim Hyung-geun**

Seoul Selection

Ask a Korean Dude

An Authoritative and Irreverent Guide to the Korea Experience

Written and compiled by **Kim Hyung-geun**

First Edition, June 2012
Revised Edition, March 2013

Published by Seoul Selection
B1 Korean Publishers Association Bldg., 105-2 Sagan-dong, Jongno-gu, Seoul 110-190, Korea
Tel: 82-2-734-9567
Fax: 82-2-734-9562
E-mail: publisher@seoulselection.com
Website: www.seoulselection.com

ISBN: 978-89-97639-00-7 03040
Printed in the Republic of Korea

For Misoon, Joohyun, and Jiryang

Contents

MAN THE HELM 47

The Korean Dude welcomes you to Korea!

KOREA: a country where tradition and rapid modernization meet in a dynamic dichotomy full of seemingly incongruous, yet somehow germane ethnic charms. It is these very elements that truly set Korea apart from its Asian colleagues as a bombastically inclined but strangely endearing little country.

Belying its "Morning Calm" name—quite possibly the biggest misnomer of the modern day—Korea is resplendent with opulent flavors, where one quaff is hardly sufficient to descry all the subtleties of over 4,000 years of culture and cultural conditioning. Indeed, Korea refuses to be ignored, blaring its presence as often as possible in the arena of the world. It chases excellence with a fervor generally reserved for starving predators hunting their prey, giving voice to secret desires for originality through the quest for unsurpassed perfection.

But to the outsider, this plethora of culture may remain esoteric at best if curiosities and questions remain unsatisfied and unanswered. To the untrained eye, ear, nose, and tongue, Korea's seeming idiosyncrasies may be difficult to digest. Fermented foods are healthy? Driving on the sidewalk? Add a year to your age? It seems unfathomable.

In an effort to break down the expatriatism of foreign versus domestic, Seoul's travel-and-culture magazine *SEOUL* launched a new channel in December of 2004 for foreigners to ask the questions about Korea they had longed to hear answered: "Ask a Korean Dude," it was called. For some years later on, loyal *SEOUL* readers actively contributed to this column, submitting poignant queries, and often relating humorous and endearing personal experiences in the process. All the while, the Korean Dude provided his deep, sincere insights, turning what were once thought of as cultural quirks into quick cultural understandings.

But the book is not just a call and response between the Korean Dude and those out of the loop with Korean culture. In fact, many fellow expatriates relate their own experiences of Korean life over the course of this book, as found in the boxes labeled "Mr./Ms. Expat Says." Though varied in content and style, each story offers a unique perspective on different topics and aspects of expat life in Korea—things that you will be sure to relate with!

So this book is ultimately an updated compilation of the Korean Dude's wisdom and a glimpse into the inner psyches of the Korean populace, as well as a venue for sharing laughs and understanding. It is a tool by which you, the foreigner, may come to not only understand the distinctly curious aspects of Korea, but also appreciate the deeply running veins of traditional and modern culture interlaced into this complex—but actually rather simple—society.

Who is the Korean Dude?

Age:	looks 30, but actually closer to 40
Sex:	male
Hair:	black, but increasingly silver
Birthplace:	Seoul
Education:	Master's degree in the US
Favorite foods:	*samgyeopsal*, kimchi and *doenjang jjigae*, spaghetti, curry, and Korean-style Chinese food
Likes:	film (Korean and foreign), modern literature, sports
Dislikes:	fur, conflicts, and liking meat
Role models:	Isaac Asimov—he has a fun and creative imagination

The Korean Dude is a droll yet insightful dude who enjoys meeting, consorting with, and observing people. He is a firm believer in the philosophy that culture has to be learned. A culture and an individual must be tamed to and by each other—just like Antoine de Saint-Exupéry's Little Prince and his Fox.

While the Korean Dude is prouder of his Korean heritage than you will know, he must confess that he often feels like a foreigner in his own country. But the Dude won't dwell on that: he is a firm believer in living the life one is given, pleasantly and well. And his theory is that learning about other cultures is a way to find what makes you happiest.

This is why the Dude likes travel, especially as a cosmopolitan who is an expert in Korean culture, but who also enjoys learning about other countries. He is not content to just watch things take place, but feels the drive to partake in and truly experience them. Thanks to his travels, the Dude likes to believe that he maintains an objective view of Korea. That way, he can better provide newcomers to Korean culture with a well-informed and well-rounded perspective on life and living in Korea.

At heart, the Korean Dude loves *makgeolli*, kimchi, *hanok* houses, and sappy television dramas, even if they are stereotypically Korean. For in the end, he is your quintessential, average-Cho Korean who just wants to share some of his Korea love.

NICE TO MEET YOU

1 GREETINGS, STRANGER

Unlike people in many English-speaking countries, where a simple "Hi" and a wave of the hand may suffice for greeting, Koreans generally observe slightly more cordial methods of salutation. Many outsiders will observe profuse of bowing, nearly superfluous expressions of deference by youngsters to elders, and other idiosyncrasies of the Joseon breed.

Many of the rules of greeting and first acquaintance stem from Korea's fundamental adherence to Confucian principles, where respect to elders is imperative and establishing one's place in the scheme of things is very important. Therefore, conveying champion breeding upon the first encounter will go a long way in facilitating your getting along in the Korean arena.

There are a few things that one may notice while cruising through high society. For one, even when another individual may not necessarily be older than or superior to oneself, Koreans generally observe a better-safe-than-sorry policy, where formal speech is used even with individuals one is certain are still attached to their mother by the umbilical cord. Also, new acquaintances will not hesitate to ask many of the questions that are typically only posed after considerable camaraderie for an ample length of time.

Confused yet? Don't know where to begin? If you'll forgive the Dude's liberal use of hyperbole, the Dude will reveal the rudiments for making a stellar first impression with Koreans. We'll begin with:

Q *How do you say "hello?"*

When greeting each other on the street, do Koreans more often say *Annyeong-hasimnikka?* or *Annyeong-haseyo?* or do they ask *Siksa hasyeot-seumnikka?* I am wondering if the "Korean for foreigners" books say it is the former because it's easier for them to adjust to, since Westerners ask "How are you?" and almost never say "Have you eaten yet?"

—STUCK ON HELLO

The Dude also prefers to say *Annyeong-haseyo?* (literally, "Are you well and at peace?"). It's easier, more ubiquitous, and, in my opinion, more appropriate. But when encountering a person around mealtime, I will occasionally ask, *Siksa hasyeot-seumnikka?* (literally, "Have you eaten?"). People usually respond, "Yes, I have," even if they haven't. Note that this greeting pattern is similar to how English speakers usually

respond to the question "How are you?" with "Fine," regardless of how they actually feel.

Despite what the Korean Dude thinks, there are many Koreans who seem to favor the gastronomic inquiry. Wondering what its significance might be....

Q *Do Koreans really need to know if I've eaten?*

I work in the evening most days of the week and am constantly asked by my students whether I have eaten dinner yet. Since

I usually don't have time to grab something before starting work, I almost always reply, "No, I haven't eaten." At first, I kind of expected an invitation to dinner; at the very least, I thought someone would hand me a piece of fruit or a candy bar—anything edible. But whenever I answer "No," I usually get a blank stare, a nod, or, in the worst cases, a smirk.

My question is this: Why do Koreans ask me whether I have had anything to eat on a regular basis, without having the slightest intention of offering me something to eat if I haven't? In the West, this would be considered somewhat rude and thoughtless. What's the point of asking me this sort of question, and what is the thought behind it?

—Hungry and Frustrated

Your question reminds me of a complaint I once read in a "Dear Ann Landers" column back in the 1980s. The question was why people didn't respond properly to "How are you?" Think of "Have you eaten dinner?" as the Korean version of "How are you?"

You may still wonder, "Why food?" A typical answer you may get from Koreans is that they suffered a lot from hunger during the Korean War and the Japanese colonial period before it. These memories still haunt their subconscious.

The Dude gives a different reason. Koreans in general consider eating to be very important. They often say, "The purpose of people doing anything is to eat." Another expression

goes, "What you eat is the only thing that you can call yours." You could say that eating is more valued in Korea than in some other cultures.

In a nutshell, Koreans are just trying to show that they care about you by asking the question, even if they don't expect any factual answer. So when you are asked, it is all right to say "Yes," even if you haven't. But as with "How are you," there are some people who sincerely wish to know that you are eating well.

The bottom line is that we should not confuse words and intentions. As you would anywhere else in the world, judge words by the way they are spoken, rather than their surface content.

Suffice it to say a simple "hello" is often insufficient to really wow your new friends. A perfectly delivered *Annyeong-haseyo?* or even *Siksa hasyeot-seumnikka?* would hardly suffice without the accompanying praxes. You are now broaching the second stage of saluting like a connoisseur: bowing. However, those new to the corporal conventions connected with introductory hailing may find the process confounding, aggravating, forbidding, and even demeaning.
Rest assured: there's an easier way to approach the gesture.

Q *When do you bow?*

I have been in Korea for quite some time and have always been confused about when and when not to bow. I know that it is an integral part of Korean, Japanese, and Chinese custom to bow in certain situations, and the rules aren't exactly the same in each country. I meet Koreans from every walk of life in both social and business situations, and I'd like to know the proper way to greet them. Sometimes someone starts to bow, and I am too slow to follow. Or I may bow, and the other person doesn't, which leaves me feeling very embarrassed.

Please let me know where I am expected to bow and where I'm not. I think this causes a lot of headaches for foreigners living and working here.

— Backache Sufferer

A It's perfectly acceptable—encouraged, in fact—to bow whenever you greet and bid farewell to somebody. You can also bow when you are introduced to somebody, while saying, "Glad to meet you." You can offer your hand for a handshake right after the bow if the person is younger than you are. Usually, the younger person greets an elder person first, and the elder person follows suit. In less formal situations, the elder person may make a half-bow.

These days, Koreans don't bow as often as they did some 20 years ago. Many are getting used to handshakes or a slighter bow, which is more of a nod of the head. You shouldn't feel embarrassed when the other person doesn't bow, because bowing can also be just a social expression of self-respect and confidence. Rest assured that no one will ever view you negatively for bowing.

 One oft-cited issue when it comes to addressing Koreans is that of titles. Unlike English-speaking countries, where the norm is to refer to others by the name of their preference (generally their first name, and generally stated outright upon first acquaintance), Korea has several different standards for referring to other people, many depending on the other person's age and rank—as well as your own—and the situation in which the individuals are seeking acquaintance.

Q *English name or Korean name?*

I am an Indian engineer working at a German engineering company. I have noticed that Koreans have a second name, which is always an English name. Koreans tend to give state this name in front of Westerners. Their real Korean name is not mentioned. Many young children in kindergarten, especially English-speaking ones, also use English names. I know many little preschoolers called Alex, Alan, Jake, Monica, and so on who use their Korean names only with friends and family.

I am happy to see Koreans being proud of their 5,000-year history. Arirang TV also mentions this. Why, then, should people be ashamed of their given Korean names, which, in a sense, represent their national and traditional identity?

—An·young

 First of all, the Dude thinks that those Koreans you met use English names not because of shame, but probably for the sake of convenience. As you may have already noticed, Westerners generally have difficulty pronouncing Korean names. Accordingly, many Koreans consider adopting an English name before they go abroad for travel, study, or business, since it can be time-consuming and (understandably) frustrating to repeatedly articulate a Korean name, particularly in urgent situations.

As for those who go willingly by English names, the Dude thinks Koreans generally want to be kind to foreigners, whom they regard as "guests." The Dude also cannot deny that some people, including kids, prefer English names partly because of the dominant cultural influence of the US.

Questions of cultural influence aside, you may wonder why some Koreans choose English names in particular, to which the Dude points out that English is currently the world's lingua franca. This also explains why Koreans are so eager and assiduous in learning English. In any case, it's not uncommon for those studying a foreign language to take a name in the target language, as this is said to help them better learn the language's sound system.

What Arirang TV declares every day is somewhat true: Korea boasts an approximately 4,300-year history (very often rounded up to 5,000). It is interesting to note that during the Japanese colonization period of Korea (1910–1945), Japan introduced a policy forcing Koreans to change their name

to a Japanese one and punishing those who refused to obey. Penalties included prohibition from entering schools and exclusion from public rationing. Despite this persecution, approximately 20 percent of Koreans still refused to change their names. Of course, digging into the political connotations behind voluntary usage of English names would raise a host of other issues. But the Dude does feel it safe to say that Koreans do maintain pride in their Korean names.

But what if you're writing someone an e-mail? Ever worried that you might be spelling someone's name wrong, or even that they may be spelling their own names wrong? Refer to the following:

Q How do you romanize Korean names?

I have lived in Korea eight years, and had the vast majority of my questions answered satisfactorily over that time. But I still don't get the Romanization of some Korean names. To wit, why did former President Roh Moo-hyun insist on his name being spelled "Roh" in Roman letters, when his name in Hangeul (노) is clearly pronounced "No." Ditto for "Lee" and "Lim," which are pronounced "Ee" and "Im," respectively. Don't Koreans feel bad being called by a name other than their own? I know the characters for the aforementioned surnames are pronounced that way in Chinese (Roh and Lee). But Koreans are not Chinese.

For many foreigners, names are an essential part of our identity. We don't want people to misuse or mispronounce our names. If the media spelled or pronounced my name incorrectly, I would ask them to correct it. So why doesn't it disturb Koreans to be called by another name?

—Spelling Dummy

You just touched upon one of the trickiest matters of the Korean language. It's called *dueumbeopchik*, a phonetic rule under which ㄹ (r) is to be pronounced and written as ㄴ (n) or ㅇ (silent) when it's used at the beginning of a word. The rule, which has been in practice since 1933, was eventually extended to the Korean spelling of family names.

Koreans don't just write their 노 (No) and 이 (Yi) names as "Roh" and "Lee" because native English speakers have gotten used to "Chinese-style" pronunciations. Originally, names like Lee and Roh were spelt with the ㄹ (l/r) sound, and changed later when South Korea updated its spelling rules. (North Korea still uses the original spellings.) But many people were unhappy with the nation's language policy, preferring to write and pronounce their names in the traditional manner as "Ro" and "Li." Recently, one family with the last name of 유 (Yoo) took the matter to court and got a verdict approving the use of "Ryu." The court ruled that forcing an individual to spell his or her name using the *dueumbeopchik* rule without considering his or her individual wishes infringes upon constitutional rights.

While the government has enforced rules on the spelling of family names in Korean, individuals have been free to choose their English spellings, which is why you will sometimes see different English spellings (for example, Lee, Rhee, or Yi) for the same name. In the case of the late Roh Moo-hyun, the Korean government specifically requested that the CIA use the President's preferred spelling of "Roh" when it was discovered that the agency's homepage was using the "No" spelling in its Korea section.

As for the family name "Choi," which is actually pronounced "Chway" in its original Korean, the deceptive spelling may have been done for the convenience of foreigners. Note that the current romanization policy of the Korean government dictates that the proper spelling of the family name "Choi" is actually "Choe."

The Dude may not be an expert linguist, but he does believe there is a delicate rule of phonetics that the sound of a language in one country is not exactly heard the same in another. Koreans can distinguish the pronunciation of certain consonants, such as the "p" (ㅍ) sound in *pul* (풀, "grass") and the "b" (ㅂ) in *bul* (불, "fire"), both of which, when spoken, sound the same as the "pp" (ㅃ) sound in *ppul* (뿔, "horn") for English-speaking people. Other examples are *tal* (탈, "mask") and *dal* (달, "moon"), both of which are often heard as *ttal* (딸, "daughter"), even though they are articulated differently.

2 A STRANGE WELCOME

Of course, greetings are not necessarily limited to hi-and-bow to Mr. or Ms. Kim, Lee, or Park. Chance dictates that you may be thrown for a loop—in fact, expect it. Not only is it a fact that everyone has their own method of introduction, but Koreans often have their own orientation when it comes to physical proximity, and even personal questions.

Be warned that many of these inadvertent, surreptitious attacks may very well ruffle your feathers and leave you reeling if you are unprepared for them. So, without further ado, the Dude presents you with a rundown of possible curveballs that may come at you.

 *Do I have to reveal my age?*

I was at a social event the other day, introducing myself to professional colleagues. I was immediately asked by a new acquaintance how old I was. Coming from the US, where there are even laws prohibiting ageism and where age is generally considered a private matter, I was a tad taken aback by this question. But when I went ahead and stated my age, I was asked to confirm my birth year, then promptly told that I was lying about my age.

What is the attitude of Koreans toward age matters? And how exactly is age calculated?

—Age-Wary

 The Korean Dude certainly understands why you would be bothered by such a question, particularly since he is getting on in years! However, the Dude would advise you not to be too offended by age-related questioning. Knowing each other's age is very important to Koreans, since relative age determines from the get-go how people will talk to and treat each other. That is, there is a specific style of honorifics, as well as a system of mannerisms, dictated by age differences between two people.

Note that, as you observed, "Korean age" is calculated differently than in Western cultures. To begin with, according

to Korean age, a baby is one year old the day they are born. This is because a person's life is seen as beginning when they are conceived. After birth, Korean age increases by one year not on a person's actual birthday, but on New Year's Day each year. This may sound ridiculous, but it means a baby born on December 31 becomes two years old the day after they are born.

Now, Koreans are also generally familiar with the Western system of measuring age, although there may be confusion, as in your particular situation. As such, people often avoid such misunderstandings by stating the year in which they were born rather than their actual age.

 *"Hello, Mr. Monkey!"*
"Okay, buddy!"

Clearly, these are "English" phrases, but I've heard Koreans (always strangers) say them to me when I'm walking down the street, hiking or visiting some other public space. It seems to be intended to make other people in a group laugh. I always thought the expressions were kind of funny myself, and seemingly innocuous. However, I always wanted to know their origin, and my Korean friends said they don't really know where they come from.

—Not a Primate

 *"Hello, hello, Mister Monkey*
You're still so fast and funky
Hello, hello, Mister Monkey
You should have been a clown"

What song comes to your mind? It's the refrain to Arabesque's hit 1977 single "Hello, Mr. Monkey." Indeed, it was in the 1980s that Western culture—including pop music—really swept into Korea. At the time, Koreans were captivated by the pop

songs flooding into Korea, with their strong beats and funky rhythms. For the obvious reason of the language barrier, the songs that became especially popular among Korean fans were those with refrains that were easy to follow. These included tunes like "Susie Q," "Funkytown," and, our favorite, "Hello, Mr. Monkey." The Korean Dude is guessing that people started calling foreigners "Mr. Monkey" because it was the only English phrase they could easily remember.

As you have witnessed firsthand, the line has been passed down to today's Korean youth. These days, popular songs from the 80s are now used in television comedy shows to represent the old days of Korea, as well as to exaggerate the rustic and naïve mood of the period.

On a related note, "buddy" is another English word that is widely known among Koreans. You do not need to speak a lot of English to know that "buddy" means "friend." Use of the word has become more widespread due to a highly popular Korean messenger program among Korean youth called "Buddy Buddy," which at one point rivaled top competitors like Nate On Messenger and Facebook. "Okay, buddy" may also have been picked up from Hollywood movies, which have had a great impact on Korean pop culture.

 *They called me a fatass!*

I am overweight, and many people like to touch or rub my stomach. Others comment on how fat I am or make suggestions on how I can lose weight. One man in the sauna actually reached over and grabbed my naked backside. He kept repeating, *Ddungddaengi* (Fatass). Is this normal behavior among Koreans, and am I just being hypersensitive about my weight being discussed? We don't openly comment on such things in America. What can I say to let someone know that my body is mine, not theirs to comment on, and certainly not

theirs to touch? I have tried getting angry and been met with stares of "I don't know why you're so angry." I have tried saying "Don't do that" in Korean, but there is little point in saying "Don't do that" after the fact.

—Cartman

I remember how when I was a child, my classmates used to tease fat boys and girls. But I've never seen Korean adults make open comments on the weight of a stranger. That's usually done "behind your back," not by "grabbing your back" or calling you "fatass"—such things are definitely considered abnormal. Those *ajeossi* (i.e. middle-aged males; their female counterparts are *ajumma*) must be far older than you, as older men tend to be less sensitive to the etiquette observed with strangers than younger Korean men are.

Of course, when friends discuss your weight and poke fun at you, it is accepted as inoffensive, since Koreans are generally less tactful with people in close relationships. But if strangers do this, you should immediately indicate that their behavior makes you upset, or else they might keep on doing it. Tell them, "I'm pissed off, you'd better apologize!" (*Gibun nabbayo, sagwahaeyo!* in Korean.) The use of slightly less formal language is an eye-for-an-eye "counter-rudeness" that emphasizes your anger and ability to stand up for yourself.

If they do say "Sorry," you will be able to alleviate the situation. However, if they don't, I would yell out (in your native language), "You have no (optional expletive here) manners!" Most Koreans will understand that much English. Above all, appear confident and be proud of your body.

If you're meeting Koreans with your children in tow, be aware that some may be more enthusiastic than others to get their hands on your little dears. Don't worry: despite initial appearances, these well-meaning older women may not necessarily be child-snatching witches. Rather, they may simply be reminiscing on their own childhood and appreciatively appraising the future generations who will carry on leading the world.

Q *Why do Korean grannies go crazy over babies?*

One of the great positives about Korea is how much Koreans adore children, and what a revered and safe place they seem to hold in society. With infants, the older Korean ladies literally go crazy. Can you explain the cultural influences behind this?

—Protective Mother

 In Korea, there is a saying that likens babies to flowers. It goes, "There is no flower more beautiful than the human flower (baby)." In an agricultural society like the Korea of some 40 years ago, the grandmother took care of kids in lieu of the mother, who was usually busy in the field. The Korean Dude assumes the time-honored tradition works in the subconscious of Koreans. If he can add one more personal impression on the matter, the rougher the experience of those grannies throughout their lives, the more fondness they show babies.

3 CAPICHE?

I t goes without saying that language can be an issue when you visit any country. But let's deal with not speaking Korean later, and talk first about speaking English in Korea. Rest assured that a vast portion of Korea's population is at least minimally educated in the basics of English speaking. Thus, foreigners generally say that it is relatively easy to travel around Seoul even for those unable to speak the native language.

But don't relax just yet. Those who converse with Koreans may soon notice the particular nuances and implications of Korean-style English. Nothing can quite prepare you for the differences in expressions and meanings, particularly when they do not make even the remotest sense.

But while the occasional linguistic encounter may hit you with shock, don't be too alarmed. Showing a touch of grace, and even administering a tactful mini-education session, will help you—and your Korean associate—go far.

Q

Why maybe?

Why do Koreans say "maybe" in odd ways? Is *ama* used differently in Korean from "maybe" in English?

Here's an example:

Teacher: *Where is your homework?*
Student: *I don't have it.*
Teacher: *Why not?*
Student: *Maybe I didn't do it.*

"Maybe"? What does he mean "maybe"? I want to reply (in my best Yoda imitation), "Did or did not. There is no maybe."

—A PadAWAN

It's true that many Koreans have trouble speaking English, especially with foreigners. Most Koreans freeze up in such situations. Even among those who are good at reading and writing, speaking fluently in English is difficult for young and old, men and women alike. In colloquial Korean, people use a lot of meaningless words and phrases like "um," "so," "well," "you know," and "maybe" when tongue-tied, just to buy time to think of something to say.

One foreign writer who speaks Korean quite well gave his

opinion on the matter of "maybe": Koreans tend to use it to death. It appears in almost any sentence that expresses any kind of uncertainty. For example, instead of saying "he might have" or "he could have," Koreans are much more comfortable saying "maybe he did."

Indeed, "maybe" is not only overused but also misused by Koreans. The student you quoted may have used it without thinking or out of habit. So teach him or her the right (non-Yoda) way to use it. If he hears the Yoda voice, he may become embarrassed and end up using the word even more often.

WHAT MR. KIM REALLY MEANT TO SAY. . .

BY DAVID KENDALL

US diplomats rate Korean as one of the hardest languages to learn, so Koreans tackling English from the other side should be commended for what they do grasp. Unfortunately, it's the oddities repeatedly heard that stick in foreign minds. Here's a guide to some common pitfalls.

Pronunciation-based Korean makes no clear distinction between p and f, v and b, l and r, s and sh, or e and i. So consider the possibility that a pair from among the usual suspects has been switched. For example, "I eat lice every day" is (hopefully) "I eat rice every day." "Where's the copy maker?" is best answered with "Do you want cream or toner with that?" Any talk of "Shitty Hall" should not be considered pejorative, unless spoken by a Seoul taxi driver. And always try replacing any "shit" you hear with "sheet" before taking offense. "Can I see that sheet?" was probably the true intention.

As for "My wife is still at work, but he will join us later," there's a far greater chance that the "he" is a "she" than that this is any declaration of an alternative lifestyle. Pronouns and plural forms are often unnecessary in Korean. Dropping "he" or "she" into an English conversation is a polite gesture. If Koreans are a letter off, so what? It's the thought that counts.

Foreigner: Didn't you send someone to meet me?
Korean: Yes.

Foreigner: No more questions?
Korean: Yes.

In both cases, "yes" most likely means "no." The Korean way is to say, respectively, "Yes (I didn't)" and "Yes (no more)." Double-check by emphasizing the "not": "Yes, you did not send someone?" "Yes, you do not have any questions?" A second "yes" definitely means "no."

Student to Foreign Teacher: I want you to change my grade.
You have to consider my effort.

In English, "I want you to…" is used when giving orders to a subordinate, but in Korean, the distinctions between "I want you to…" "Could you…?" and "I'd like you to…" are made with suffixes, not different words. Most Koreans are unaware how "I want you to…" sounds because they learned (correctly) that English has none of the "polite" and "low" forms found in languages like Korean and German. But many have also incorrectly learned that "should" and "have to" are the same.

> *Foreigner: How are you?*
> *Korean: Fine, thank you, and you? or Good.*

The problem is not just rote memorization. It is the combination of hackneyed phrases and a locally cherished flat tone that leaves Koreans sounding like aliens trying to infiltrate our world. Keep in mind that English tones sound feminine or emotional to some speakers of other languages, so there's not always a strong desire to "sound natural" in English.

Things like those above are easily overlooked and deciphered by both sides: Many newcomers, myself included, have told taxi drivers *Yeogi juseyo* ("Please give me here") instead of the more correct *Yeogiyo* or *Yeogi sewo juseyo*. And "this year" is never *i nyeon*, though Koreans are often too polite to tell you what you really said with this.

Culture-based confusion causes the most consternation, with queries such as "How old are you?" or "Where are you going?" Both are reflexive translations of routine Korean inquiries. Simple responses like "older/younger than you" or "I'd rather not say" for age and "to meet someone" or "someplace" for destinations will sweep them away. People expect no more sincerity than English speakers do when asking a casual acquaintance, "How are you?"

In Korea, there may also be times when you want to be cautious about which language you decide to speak with the locals, even if you are multilingual. Choose your time and place well:

Q *Does speaking English hurt national pride?*

I am a journalist from Nepal who is studying the Korean language at a Korean university. As a journalist, I want to do a lot of news reports about Korea and its array of social and economic issues, but I have found the language to be the main barrier in communicating with people and getting the desired information. I've been bewildered to have even people in top positions answer my written questions in Korean. Do they really not speak English, or are they just pretending they don't so as to "forcefully" focus on Korean?

—Missing English

A

In most cases, the Korean Dude guesses, they prefer the Korean language for reasons of precision, especially when

they are talking to the press. They may think that their written English is not good enough for official purposes. Ranks are not necessarily associated with English skills here in Korea. Next time, you may be better off forgetting the written questionnaire if you'd like them to speak to you in English.

MAN THE HELM

1 METROPOLITAN MAYHEM

A mong the first things the new Korea arrival encounters is the absolute chaos that often accompanies navigation of the streets of big cities, especially Seoul. On the one hand, this may seem unsurprising, since Seoul (one of the world's largest cities) plays host to over 10 million residents, accounting for about one-fifth the total population of South Korea.

But, as you may soon realize, the conditions of the urban jungle cannot be attributed entirely to density. We're talking about a country full of speeders and the grim-faced, not to mention people with no qualms about getting up close and personal.

Roadrunners zipping in every direction, not afraid to crash into you like a pinball—now that makes for a uniquely Korean experience.

 *Why the hurry?*

Why are locals always so eager to disembark from an airplane before it even lands on the tarmac? Every time my wife and I are on a plane back to Incheon, locals will jump out of their seats shortly after the plane lands, while the foreigners remain seated and wait for the seatbelt signs to go off. And why don't the flight attendants do anything about it?

—Curious Flyer

 Probably the same reason that foreigners are sometimes shocked by the reckless driving of the cab drivers here who feel free to zoom through red lights. It's an often embarrassing trait of contemporary Koreans to get things done as quickly as possible—if not too quickly. This is otherwise known as the *ppalli ppalli* ("quickly, quickly!") phenomenon.

It is true that Korea is a very fast-paced society, particularly in the capital city of Seoul. This hurrying is not only apparent in the fast strides of pedestrians on the street, but also in the speed of public transportation, business transactions, and even mail delivery. There may be a million reasons that people feel the need to rush around all the time, but the main one seems to stem from post-war Korea, when the nation was in a rush to

modernize and industrialize.

Korea certainly has the results to show for its efforts: in just 30 years, it grew from a third-world country to the 15th largest economy in the world.

But the Dude hears what you are saying: society as a whole should be better at slowing down and following the rules. For example, Koreans shouldn't jump out of their seats before their seatbelt signs go off—for safety reasons, if nothing else. And while the flight attendants are probably busy with other things during landing, they seem to be far too used to passengers preemptively preparing for exit to do anything about it. Or maybe there are just too many for them to bother!

THE UNBEARABLE LIGHTNESS OF SMILING

BY JUNE KIM

I am appalled at how little smiling goes on in Seoul. Although residents of large metropolises the world over are famously unfriendly, I must say that Seoulites seem the unfriendliest of them all. My mother tells me that elders scolded her for flashing a smile while walking down the aisle at her wedding. They didn't say why you shouldn't smile on what is supposed to be the happiest day of your life, but she gathered that they considered it to make light of a serious and solemn occasion. This leads me to believe that even though smiling is universally accepted as a sign of happiness, acceptance, understanding, and friendliness, it can also (in Korea, at least) be regarded as an expression of belittlement or lack of commitment, seriousness, or resolve. Be that as it may, Koreans, for all their reluctance to give smiles, do not seem to mind receiving them. I got a significant discount on a pair of shoes at a Dongdaemun market by using my version

of a "Julia Roberts smile," and I was offered a few extra dumplings at a street stall by impressing the *ajumma* there. Ask not how many smiles this country can give you, but how many you can give this country.

 *Left, right . . . or center?*

When walking around the city, I am never sure which side of the sidewalk to use. Public areas have signs indicating that we should stick to the right. But do people really abide by this rule? If I keep to the left, I appear to be in the wrong. Then I try to keep to the right, but I still end up having to dodge people who are walking toward me. Even if I veer to the center of the sidewalk, I'm still in trouble. So, Korean Dude, is there some unwritten code here? Do we pedestrians just walk on whichever side of the path we want?

—Stuck on the Sidewalk

 Let me explain the source of the confusion first. Under Japanese colonial rule, every vehicle and pedestrian was supposed to travel on the left side of the road. But after Korea's liberation in 1945, vehicles began driving on the right, following the lead of US military vehicles, while pedestrians remained on the left. Until recently, schools taught kids to walk on the left.

But now Korea's National Police Agency has revised traffic law once and for all, switching the direction of walking to the right in keeping with international practice. The change was based on expert findings that keeping to the left goes against nature. According to the study, fully 73 percent of people

preferred keeping right. The change in direction is expected to increase walking speed nearly twofold and minimize crashes between pedestrians and traffic.

Most civilians are having a difficult time adjusting to the abrupt introduction of this new rule, and many continue to walk in either direction, particularly during rush hours. But do try to stick to the right as much as possible.

 *What happened to my bubble?*

Many people who come from smaller cities in the West, as I do (population 100,000), may not believe that walking in Seoul is much different than walking in their own city. I beg to differ. Crowds aside, it seems that Korean people don't mind being bumped into or bumping into other people. On streets and in social situations, they also do not seem to have any reservations about invading your personal space, or just generally feeling at liberty to touch or otherwise come into physical contact with you. This often makes me very uncomfortable. What are the rules in Korea when it comes to physical proximity?

—Craving SOME Room

A Koreans do tend to be less reserved when it comes to physical proximity. Foreigners may be unfamiliar with the sight of grown men holding hands and girls walking together with their arms around each other's waist. It is not seen as particularly unusual to bump into people—despite various public awareness campaigns, such as can be viewed on subway television screens—and offenders do not always apologize.

One must be aware that culturally, Koreans do not observe the concept of the "personal bubble"—that fixed distance maintained between a person and the others surrounding them. This is at least partly due to Korea being a very heavily populated yet geographically small nation. The Dude has found that politely requesting more space generally garners positive results. However, some natives may find the request offensive, if only because of the rarity of someone being so straightforward. In other cases, the other person will craftily revert back to what he or she was doing in the first place.

As much as possible, it is wise to try and maintain a certain distance from others. However, if they do end up touching you, there's not much else you can do but try not to flinch. Some Koreans seem to have developed a habit of "caving in" their body weight on impact and reducing the pain of a collision.

DR. STREET SMART, OR HOW I LEARNED TO STOP WORRYING AND LOVE THE CROWDS

BY ELIZABETH SHIM

It's happened to the best of us at least once. You tried to smile, mask your indignation, and feign nonchalance. "Wait!" your instincts said. "That nice-looking lady just elbowed you in the ribs and is now lounging sans regret in the seat you've been eying for the last five stops!" Or maybe you're in line, groceries in tow, momentarily admiring the fine rack of triple-A batteries by the counter. Before you know it, the otherwise dignified gentleman behind you is happily inching up to your place in line.

From time to time when you live in Seoul, it just seems like, even when you're not snoozing, you're losing out to the competitive pedestrian/ grocery shopper and "I need to be first in everything" mentality that afflicts Seoul urbanites today. Is there any solution to this predicament, which causes such woe to the unanointed? The following are some aberrant behaviors that can and do go unchecked in the subways. Chances are, you've seen one of each on a weekly basis at least. This column aspires to berate, amuse, and offer some unfinalized answers to all your commuting tribulations—but, as always, discretion is advised.

1. THE NEWSPAPER READER

Completely unpardonable, but there he is (and yes, it's usually a man). You enjoy having personal space (who doesn't?), but he forgets that you do, largely because he thinks your space is just as good as his, and mi casa es su casa, so hey, why not indulge in a little neighborly

hospitality? Without a second thought, he unfolds a major daily and, next thing you know, you're seeing the latest headlines on page 12 as the scent of newsprint hits your nostrils. Add to this interesting conundrum his penchant for sitting with his legs apart like a compass—now you're not just sharing reading material, you're also sharing seats. Solution? Send a few subtle signs of displeasure his way. If he doesn't catch the signals, try whiling away the commuting minutes catching up on the latest headlines (provided you can read Korean) as he holds the paper up for your viewing convenience.

2. THE STARER

This one may be a no-brainer, especially if you're accustomed to traveling in countries where your presence offers a dash of the unusual. But even in the Korean lexicon, staring at foreign folk just isn't acceptable. The country is actively adopting global standards of etiquette, and a growing number of people are studying, traveling or working overseas. In sum, most Koreans do not find you as peculiar as you might think, unless that Korean is a starer. The starer comes in two varieties. Type X is usually an unassuming "frog in the well" personality who is in shock and awe at your very presence. He will stare relentlessly, wide-eyed (and, at times, slack-jawed) and without a hint of shame. Type Y, on the other hand, is a bit more guarded and (often being a woman) gives male commuters a hard time if even the briefest eye contact is made, emitting a very strong "stay away" message in bold type without uttering a single word. Solution? Direct eye contact is often intended to provoke and easily misinterpreted. Save yourself some oxygen and don't stare back.

3. THE SLEEPER

This rider comes in two distinct flavors: tolerable and intolerable. The tolerable is a seasoned snoozer with built-in reflexes that let her snap back into position whenever she swerves off-center. She strides the fine line between sublime slumber and cognizant awareness. The intolerable, on the other hand, takes no cues, or doesn't know how. Guide her back into position and there she is again, reclining on you, her human pillow of choice. Come her stop, she takes a look around, shrugs off the annoyed look on your face, and takes off, with nary a hint of apology. Solution? By all accounts, the intolerable sleeper is a poster girl for unacceptable behavior. If your responses of vexation don't go through, you can either report her to the authorities or let her go. Let her go, that is, unless you're looking for a date and she has what you're looking for.

4. THE UNAPOLOGETIC PUSHER

Not exactly trying to save the best for last, but this is, without a doubt, the most aggravating archetype of civic-mindlessness. The pusher is not confined to the subway. He's found on crowded streets, in shopping malls, and in ticket lines. Add to his formidable aggression his fearlessly unapologetic outlook, and you've got yourself a case of culture shock. The pedigree of the pusher is unknown; most experts date his origins to mid-20th century Korea, when food was scarce, rationed, and distributed on a first-come, first-served basis. While we cannot be completely sure where he came from, we do know, he's getting wherever he's going faster than you. Solution: Brush off the experience and turn your attention to the curvature of your nails—or, better yet, plans for the Chuseok holidays. And never forget: some people really are in a hurry, and for a very good reason. Including, of course, finding the nearest bathroom.

2 KOREAN WOMEN

I f Korean society at large is intriguing to you, Korean women may be an area of study all their own. Here is a unique brand of individual so colorful that it warrants "I love" lists the world over on the pukka Korean lady. (One particular Internet phenomenon entitled "why keeping Korean women happy is worth it" comes to mind. . . .)

Rest assured, Korean women may be, collectively, one of the most resilient groups of people you will ever meet. Fighting against centuries of Confucian oppression, Korean women of the 20th century fought tooth and nail not only to alter their roles within the family, but also to distinguish themselves in the academic and professional arenas. Women now compete with their male counterparts in every area of society and business. Of course, education has also resulted indirectly in a dramatic decline in fertility, with Korea placing as the world's sixth-least fertile country in the world in 2011.

Despite increased standards, however, you will find (as in any other country) peculiarities demonstrated by certain members of the female sex, all with a characteristically Korean touch.

Do young Korean women have a phobia of pigeons?

Whenever I am walking on the street, young women (anywhere from students to 20-somethings) will act very flustered if there are pigeons about. They seem to be somewhat scared and avoid the birds, doing whatever it takes not to go anywhere near them. The high-pitched little scream that appears to accompany this behavior becomes somewhat annoying after a while—after all, they are only pigeons. I have seen little children frolicking around pigeons and having lots of fun. The young women, however, act as though the world is about to cave in. Are they just being "cute," hoping some "knight in shining armor" will come rescue them from the pigeons? Or is there really some kind of superstition or logical reason for this behavior?

—Bert's Sister

There are no traditional superstitions against pigeons. The Dude thinks that only some young women are very scared of pigeons—though no one really seems to like the birds, either. Personally, the Dude hasn't witnessed men avoiding them out of fear.

Negativity toward pigeons may have something to do with a widely viewed pigeon-related hygiene report that was aired on television some years ago. In addition to lice, pigeons have been known to carry flu- and pneumonia-like diseases. According to the report, pigeons flying overhead can potentially drop bacteria and viruses onto you. Also, spores from pigeon droppings can supposedly be carried on the wind and eventually inhaled.

It probably doesn't help that the bodily wastes that inevitably come with rapidly proliferating pigeon populations are known to erode the roofs of valued cultural monuments such as palaces and temples. Many of the Dude's friends also say that they feel disgusted when they see pigeons eating garbage or vomit.

As to your guess about women trying to be "cute," the Dude can't answer that. Perhaps young girls see their friends scream and automatically follow suit. As for why Korean men don't seem to be flustered by pigeons, perhaps it's because guys stereotypically have higher tolerance for filth than women. Or maybe they just don't want to appear cowardly over a small bird!

 ## Q *Why do ladies dress like Muslims?*

I am curious about two things in Korea: people wearing white gloves for just about anything (even when walking down the street or putting items out for display in a store), and Korean women (usually *ajummas*) wearing hideous sun visors, clipping white towels around them, and even sporting a white mask in the front, so that they almost look like devout Muslim women.

I realize the ozone layer isn't what it used to be, and skin cancer is more prevalent these days, but it strikes me that most Korean women seem to want to stay oh-so-white. This is odd, coming as it does amid a push to accept people who are different, especially multicultural Koreans who are sometimes

dark-skinned. Why do so many Koreans fear getting a suntan? Down here in Jeollanam-do where I live, I've met some Koreans who are in fact tan, and they look fine to me.

—Sun Bather

The emphasis on white skin doesn't seem to be strongly related to racial perceptions—white skin was glorified long before Koreans were even aware of the different skin colors of other races. Rather, darker skin was traditionally linked to the lower classes, since farmers who worked in the sun all day would naturally have very tan skin. By the same token, pale skin was traditionally considered more of a high-class look, since nobles, who did not see so much sun, would have much lighter skin than the lower classes.

But race does seem to play some part in this obsession with pale. Culturally and traditionally, Koreans have been strong advocates of endogamy and marrying within their race. In the Korean Dude's experience, there seems to be an association between dark skin and foreigners.

Add to this a desire to look perfect at all times—the plethora of skin clinics throughout urban Korea is good proof of this—and you've got a recipe for full coverage. Of course, modern science also tells us that sun exposure is more likely to result in wrinkles later in life, so many women are naturally afraid of skin troubles problems due to sun exposure.

While donning cotton gloves in the workplace or while driving seems to be more characteristic of older women, the end goal of preventing premature skin problems and calluses—as well as splotchy tanning—remains the same. Softer hands are also believed to enhance one's femininity.

Ajumma refers to middle aged, married women. If you've been to Korea for even the shortest time, you've no doubt seen them: brows permanently furrowed, hair like ramyeon, and a remarkable ability to make their way through Seoul's thick crowds. They are unafraid to tell you what they think (sometimes doing so quite loudly), and possess a near legendary frugality that would make the IMF proud. Voila, you have spotted the ever-iconic *ajumma*.

Q *Why do moms let kids pee in public places?*

Occasionally, I've noticed children with their mothers pause, look around, and then suddenly pull down their pants and begin to urinate. This even occurs in places like parks and streets! How come I'm the only one who thinks this is strange?

—Not Amused

Nowadays, fewer and fewer people relieve themselves in public, but many still do. They simply think that others will understand. They would rather do their business where it is convenient than take the trouble to find bathrooms. In general, it's not socially condemned. This probably developed when Korea was an agricultural society, which was not all that long ago. Farmers at that time used human muck for fertilizer. You may know that the Korean word for "fertilizer" is often used as a verb to mean "excrete." When parents let their kids pee in a vegetable field, they used to say they were "fertilizing the field." Another belief is that children's urine can be used as medicine. Some pharmaceutical companies collect urine for this purpose.

Ms. Expat Says...

IN DEFENSE OF *AJUMMAS*

BY YOUNGHI SEO

Most people find the average middle-aged, married Korean woman too loud and aggressive. And in a patriarchal society that values femininity, beauty, and (increasingly) youth, *ajumma* is thought to be unattractive—"loud," even, with their fashion and manner—which is considered damn near criminal in a country that boasts some of the best-looking women in the world. Sometimes referred to as "the third sex," *ajumma* are regarded as uncosmopolitan at best, uncouth at worst. Personally, I think *ajumma* has a bad rap.

Everywhere in these crowded, chaotic streets of Seoul, I see *ajumma*. Now, the mayor may think he rules this city, but it's the *ajumma* who are really running the show. For instance, consider the "miraculous" economic development of Korea—could it have happened without the *ajumma*? I remembering reading once that the people who do the world's real work usually don't wear neckties. Here in Korea, the ones doing the real work are the middle-aged women laboring in restaurants, shops, factories, schools, offices, apartment buildings, and even in the streets as vendors. These women are also the ones who provided Korea with its current educated and skilled labor force.

Once, an older female friend told me that a woman turns into a tigress when she has children. In order to protect and provide for her young, she will do anything, and without hesitation. Her keen powers of observation

(based on personal experience) stayed with me. I thought about *ajumma*,
especially those who raised their children during the late 1960s and 1970s.
These were lean, tough decades in Korea's history. For the current *ajumma*
who was young mothers then, and had been raised during the war and
reconstruction, the memory of poverty and deprivation must have seemed
very real. This motivated them to grow tough and work hard. Conditioned

by a competitive environment, the *ajummas* drove their children to study hard and pushed themselves, and often their spouses, to be more productive. Many of them, including my own mother, even summoned the courage to immigrate to other countries, where they endured terrible hardship.

I'm a bit awestruck by the attitude of *ajummas*. There is a strong survival instinct in these women, a "can-do" attitude—which, interestingly enough, seems less developed in younger generations. Women my age tend to think too much, especially the more educated among us. For example, say a coworker, or even a friend, offended us. We mull it over for a while, gauging our emotions and wondering how to respond. And the women of my mother's generation? They don't think about it. They don't hesitate. They cut the offending person down with a cold stare or a few choice words. Or else they just get over it.

So, in the end, I admire and like *ajummas* for the same reason I prefer Koreans from the countryside (as opposed to Seoulites): most are honest and direct, often unassuming and unapologetic in their straightforwardness. They say you shouldn't judge someone unless you've walked a mile in her shoes. The streets of Seoul and the rest of the country are paved with the efforts of *ajummas*, and I sometimes wonder if we haven't taken them for granted or acted downright disrespectful.

Sooner or later, I will be an *ajumma* myself. I only hope that I can do the current *ajumma* proud and follow in her strong foot-steps, with the same honesty, integrity, and courage she's shown me.

3 VEHICULAR VISIONS·

 It seems safe to say that Korea has a very unique driving culture to say the least. Koreans have a reputation for adventurous driving, a reputation that is arguably well earned, even if things have improved greatly over the last couple of years. If you learned to drive in a more tranquil road culture, getting used to Korean roads may take some time getting used to. But that what the Korean Dude is here for—to help you get started.

Q *Why the dull car colors?*

Something I noticed on my first trip here in 2003, and just take for granted now that I've lived in Seoul for a year, is the dull colors of cars on the road here in Korea: black, black, black, black, black, white, and silver. Elsewhere, I've seen Hyundais and KIAs in bright yellows and reds, but not here. The other night I saw a metallic crimson Lexus in Yeoksam-dong, and I heard someone had his Equus resprayed fire engine red (both probably belonging to expats). So, esteemed Korean Dude, why are the cars here so dull and conformist in color?

—Bored with these Wheels

Broadly speaking, Koreans stick to simple colors. Ironically, they are choosing these shades to distinguish themselves.

It's true that black is preferred by the rich and the powerful. It's a good color for those who want to differentiate themselves from the masses. They think black can lend dignity, with its heavy and serene tone. White and silver are also beloved, probably for the same reason. Businesspeople here tend to think that colors like yellow, red, and blue are not good for serious matters. Secretly, many Koreans are wary of sticking out.

Another point is that cars are one of the few things that indicate social class. This is the very reason that Koreans are so crazy about foreign cars, even though they are three to ten times more expensive than regular rides. It should also be pointed out that the more authoritarian a society is, the more it

shows a preference for drab colors. Democracy is a rather new experience in Korea, after all. As a car owner, the Dude might point to other more practical reasons: if you want your car in a unique color scheme, it takes forever to get it repainted.

 *What's the deal with parking?*

It seems that Koreans park anywhere: on the sidewalk, in the highway merge lane, and three deep on the street. But I got a ticket when I parked on the side of a wide street!

—Circling the Block

 Many Koreans do have the tendency to act according to convenience rather than law. But it's also a fact that there's a definite lack of parking space in cities. What is there is well short of accommodating the burgeoning houses and people in the wake of rapid urbanization. Speaking from my own experience, things have gotten a lot better recently in terms of both parking spaces and law-abiding spirit with traffic surveilance cameras. Sorry, but I'm afraid it will take some time for the situation to be completely corrected.

Q *Are there no rules for motorcycles?*

Do you need a license to drive a motorcycle in Korea? And what are the rules for the Ministry of Transportation in Korea? I ask because I constantly see bikes riding on the sidewalk, running red lights, and carrying three people at once. Not to mention the lack of helmets and the fumes they spew. Why are the rules of the road not enforced?

—Disgruntled Pedestrian

A Yes, you need a license to drive a motorcycle. Those who have a driver's license are allowed to ride a motorcycle with up to 125 cc displacement. Those who don't need to get a license if they want to drive a motorcycle. In order to drive larger bikes, you have to take a written test and field test. Motorcyclists without helmets are subject to fines, as are those who drive on the sidewalk. The Dude once caught a pizza delivery guy and yelled at him for driving wildly in an apartment complex. According to the police, a fine of 1,000,000 won to 2,000,000 won is levied on those who drive a motorcycle without a license, and 20,000 won if they aren't wearing a helmet. The Dude also sees eye to eye with you on police enforcement of traffic laws not being strict enough. The Dude even asked the Jongno Police Station about it. An officer in the relevant department said strict enforcement "might cause accidents, especially if young kids try to escape from the cops for fear of being caught." Just for your reference, those 16 or over can apply for a motorcycle license, and those 18 or over can get a driver's license.

TRAFFIC CONFUCIAN IN SEOUL

BY DAVID KENDALL

"When two cars enter opposite ends of a road reduced to one lane by illegally parked cars, the older driver shall have the right of way. Should the younger driver's car be markedly more expensive and powerful, however, the older driver should yield." Were I to write a traffic manual based on my five years of driving experience in Seoul, this would be one of the entries. But the rules keep changing, and even foreigners are expected to follow the letter of the law nowadays. "Sir, you cannot make a U-turn on a red light!" barked the KATUSA-turned-Robo-Traffic-Cop who flagged me down on my once-routine drive home. Police used to wave *oeguk saram* (foreigners) through breathalyzer roadblocks. Now, everyone is expected to play by the rules, and both statistics and personal observation show the crackdown is paying off.

For someone coming from a multi-cultural society, Korea's homogeneity in terms of things like wholesale disregard for traffic rules can be taxing, but it's also fun to witness things jar Korea's collective conscience enough to cause a tectonic shift in social etiquette. Examples of this include the heat wave of '94, when *ajeossi* nationwide pulled down centuries of orthodoxy and stepped out in shorts for the first time, or the pre-World Cup campaign that has left one side of escalators free and parted crowds long enough to allow subway passengers to exit cars. Once again, millions are heeding a call to change all at once. On Seoul's streets, more and more people are modifying their driving. Professors Yang Bong-min and Kim Jin-hyun found that in just over a year before the 2002 World Cup, government fines and media-sponsored public awareness campaigns brought the percentage of Koreans buckling up from 23 to 98, one of the highest rates in the world.

In terms of traffic fatalities per 100,000 citizens, Korea is still among the OECD's worst performers, but it bodes well that those statistics are posted on the Road Traffic Authority (KoROAD)'s website (http://eng.koroad.or.kr/Eng/Main/main.jsp), and Korea's rate has plummeted to levels on par with the United States. Officialdom is making a concerted effort to try new ideas and measure effectiveness to improve living standards. To reduce air pollution and congestion, the city is pushing a voluntary campaign to get commuters to leave their cars at home one day a week. Anyone who registers receives a sticker proclaiming their day of abstinence. This campaign, which is running in Seoul, Gyeonggi-do, Incheon, Daegu, and Busan, reduces taxes for registered vehicles and entitles drivers to benefits at various public institutions. It is also open to foreign residents.

Foreigners can drive in Seoul on a valid international license for up to a year. Long-term residents, however, should obtain a Korean license, an easy process detailed on the city's website (http://english.seoul.go.kr). The KoROAD has also issued its own "Manual for Safe Driving for Foreigners." In it, you'll learn how those involved in small accidents generally try to reach a settlement on the spot. Even with serious wrecks, Koreans often strive for a settlement, throwing out a wide net of friends and acquaintances in hopes of catching someone who has influence with the victim's family.

While the KoROAD manual stresses things like the injurer and victim's responsibility to "observe decorum from a moral point of view," you won't

find any mention of blind spots. Apparently, Korean *nunchi* (the ability to detect others' intentions) extends to peripheral vision. A Korean friend once warned me not to check my blind spot: "I learned that in America, too. But forget it here. Traffic moves too fast and tight in Seoul." I brushed the advice aside as if it were one more Korean urban myth, like the people who suffocate while sleeping with the fan on and windows closed. To my chagrin, though, my only accident here was caused by my own blind spot check. I haven't found any office that tracks the number of foreigners who wreck as a result of "failure to resist checking their blind spot," but I suspect I wouldn't be the sole figure in that column. I'll never have strong enough *nunchi* or faith enough in those tiny dash-mounted mirrors to switch lanes without a glance, but they are much more fleeting now.

Driving is exciting these days because I sense another of Korea's overnight facelifts coming. Any day now, I'm going to wake up and find drivers stopping when lights turn red, moving to the side of the road for ambulances, and maybe even letting other cars into their lanes when they signal instead of speeding up to block them. People in heterogeneous societies may be more careful not to step on each other's toes, but I admire the way Koreans can take giant steps together.

Q

What are these trucks spewing white smoke?

On my first day in Korea, I was sitting in a bakery, having a leisurely breakfast, when a truck made its way slowly down the road, spewing thick white smoke from a batting machine-type device. My first thought was "chemical weapons." I was perfectly petrified for a few seconds. I looked to the staff of the bakery to see if they had noticed, but their faces were absent of horror, and my reasoning eventually caught up with my impulses. Now I know that these are sanitation trucks and that they have something to do with mosquito control. That's all well and good. But what exactly is that white smoky stuff that I inhaled?

—Smoked

A

You must have been very surprised to see that first sanitation truck! But Koreans are quite used to this vehicle spewing its stinky white gas. In the 1970s and the 1980s, children who had nothing else to play with would rush over to be enveloped by the smoke trailing from the back end of the truck. After a while, some of them would find themselves ending up in a strange part of town. In the 1970s, one of the most important epidemic prevention projects involved sterilization. The sanitation truck

started patrolling to exterminate vermin, insects, parasites, roundworms, and so forth. The gas is made up of insecticide, along with other ingredients for wiping out pests. The gas isn't deadly, but it's not exactly good for your health. According to a 2003 study, the concentration of bad gases like ozone, sulfurous acid, nitrogen dioxide, and carbon monoxide was found to be higher and more dangerous than usual after spraying. So I recommend you avoid the truck, shut your window, and wait until it passes by if you meet the sanitation truck again. On the other hand, maybe it's not so bad to just sit there and meditate, imagining that you're a hermit in the smoggy clouds.

Q
What's with the police car roof flashers?

Please tell me why police cars in Korea keep their roof flashers on all the time. My European conditioning still causes me to react with alarm when I see those lights, or even pull over if I am driving. But I have seen a patrol car parked peacefully at night on a quiet side street, two equally peaceful officers fast asleep inside, engine running, and all the while with those revolving strobes bathing the neighborhood in blue light waves. In my country, these lights indicate an emergency. Are the Korean police "crying wolf," or are we just in a constant state of crisis?

—Smooth Criminal

A

As you already know, patrol cars are used to prevent crimes and deal with emergencies. The car's structure is no different from other conventional vehicles; what makes it unique is its siren and roof lights. These are supposed to be used only in urgent situations. That is what the principle prescribes. But we have received a slightly more liberal definition of "emergency." The officers at the police station near our office said their daily work guidelines advise them to keep the flashers on when patrolling at night in order to prevent crimes and raise people's awareness. Not many patrol cars put on their lights during the daytime. You don't have to pull over when a patrol car passes you with its lights on, unless the officer actually sounds their siren or calls out your license number through their speaker. So the rule is no siren, no worries.

In fact, police are actually told *not* to turn on their sirens or flashers in emergencies, so as to avoid preemptively alerting criminals they are trying to ambush.

4 THE BIZARRE

Korea is talented at theatrics, and not only with those thrilling television dramas that are all the rage across Asia and overseas. One walk down a street lit all bright and crazy with neon will illuminate just a smattering of the peculiarities to be found in Korea.

From rampant trend worshipping and prosaic panhandlers to sketchy signage and services—paying even a little attention to all the elements around you should provide plenty of entertainment for anyone's eyes.

Of course, not all is as blatantly unattractive as that list might make Korea seem. Even a brief look behind the topics listed reveals that there are some very interesting back stories to be considered before you pass judgment.

While Korea holds countless peculiarities—peculiar either because you are unfamiliar with Korea, or because something is just plain strange (or both!)—and the Korean Dude could not possibly hope to explain them all, he will have a go at some of them in the following pages.

 ## *Walking with hands behind back = comfortable?*

While walking the streets of Seoul, I've often witnessed elderly Koreans walking with their hands behind their backs. Younger Koreans don't seem to display this same preference for hand placement. Why do older Koreans do this?

—Puzzled Youth

 The Dude only can guess that it has to do with the walking habits of the ruling aristocratic class, or *yangban*, of the Joseon period. Scholars or government officials, the *yangban* were taught to stay calm and unbiased spiritually and physically even when required to respond quickly. They were told to walk with dignity and advised not to scurry, lest they lose mental and physical balance in front of the ruled. The Dude wasn't taught to walk that way—the concept of the *yangban* departed with the Joseon era—but he does find it comfortable, especially when walking in a pensive mood. It would be somewhat funny to see foreigners walk like *yangban*, but give it a try if you feel like it. After all, different cultural behaviors can be better understood through experience.

Q *Why do people panhandle the same way?*

Are the majority of panhandlers in Korea truly needy people? How much support do they get from the government and charities? I ask because I see panhandlers everywhere doing exactly the same things: old people selling gum, women holding white boxes, and men with black rubber on their legs crawling around on a kind of skateboard. They look needy, but why do they approach people in exactly the same way?

—Cautious Empath

The Dude never really thought about this until you asked. But given the various panhandling methods employed by the American indigent, including the squeegee technique and holding up signs reading "will work for food," the Dude now admits there are probably many ways to get the job done. As you described it, Korean panhandlers are less talkative, and therefore less communicative with their donors. What underlies the approach of Korean panhandlers, the Dude guesses, is a sense of shame. You've no doubt noticed that most of them will not look you in the eyes. For professional reasons, it's also important that they look as pathetic as possible. The government does provide some camp-like shelters for the homeless, but the Dude has heard that many panhandlers are loath to sacrifice their freedom for food and a bed. It should also be noted that many are not technically homeless, but merely poor, and beg to supplement their meager income.

 *V for victory?*

I've noticed this with Japanese people, too, but many Koreans instinctively raise two fingers in a peace sign for the camera when they have their picture taken. At first, I just thought it was a silly gesture. But then I noticed that nearly every picture would feature at least one person wishing peace upon the picture-taker! I kid. But why do so many young people make a "V" sign with their fingers when they are being photographed?

—Puzzled Foreigner

 As you may already know, Winston Churchill made the "V" sign famous during World War II, though he didn't create it. Koreans were, of course, exposed to Churchill's photographs.

But there is one more reason. If the Dude's memory serves him correctly, there was a very famous cartoon or TV show called *The Sign Is V* back in the 70s. You can still find people on the Internet saying *Yeoksi saineun beuiya* ("The 'V' sign is still the best").

with friends...

ANT ARMY:
KOREA'S COLLECTIVE INDIVIDUALITY

BY JUNE KIM

There is a preconceived notion that East Asians, most notably the Japanese and Koreans, have a tendency and desire to conform to the values, beliefs, and behavior of the majority. And, indeed, this notion is not without its truth.

Hair dyeing has been a perennial trend in Korea. Since the early 90s, lightening your hair color to a radical shade of blond has been the "in" thing, although its popularity has been waning somewhat in the past few years. When asked why they chose their color, and why they dyed their hair at all, almost everyone with an uncomfortably blond weave will tell you it is because of their individuality.

It is a strange kind of individuality—one that every other Korean seems to have. Going to a hair salon in Korea can be a tiring experience for those of us who do not care for the latest trends. Many Korean hairdressers have chastised me for asking for a cut that was not trendy: "Nobody gets their hair cut like that these days. You have to get a shag cut/some highlights/a perm."

The hairdressers are obviously just trying to make more money by nudging me toward a more expensive style. What surprises me, though, is their assumption that they can convince me to style my hair differently by telling me that what I want is not what everyone else is getting.

The same logic is prevalent in the bartering techniques of market vendors: "It looks great on you. It's the latest trend. Oh, no, I can't give it to you for that price. This is what everyone is wearing, after all." The fact that consumer psychology is based on what everyone else has or does says a lot about the Korean collective consciousness.

And this consumer psychology reflects and explains such concepts as the *wangtta* (outcast) and *twida* (to stand out). A person who behaves, talks, or dresses in a manner that makes them *twida* could become a *wangtta* and be shut out of peer groups and social circles.

Groupthink is also evident in food, drink, and even health food trends. As an expatriate who comes to Korea every few years, my mother was baffled on her last visit to note that she was having a difficult time finding a particular line of aloe-based health care products that had been extremely popular the last time she had been there. She asked my aunt, who had used the same products. Amused, my aunt responded, "Nobody uses those any more. It is no longer the trend."

Experienced expatriate travelers in Korea are undaunted by the familiar summer news footage of Haeundae Beach—the most famous beach in Busan, and Korea as a whole—or Seoraksan Mountain overflowing with zealous vacation crowds. They say that if you walk just a little way out of the way from the most famous beach or hiking trail, you will always find a tranquil, secluded spot, simply due to the tautological fact that practically no one goes there. This is a particularly bizarre (and personally welcome) manifestation of the Korean penchant for conformity—I am relieved to know that I do not need to be a speck in a wave of humans competing for leisure time and space if I do make my way to a popular travel destination this summer.

While conformity does have a generally negative connotation, Koreans' tendency to conform, known as the *gaemi gundan* ("ant army")

phenomenon, plays a vital role in sustaining and improving certain sectors of the domestic economy. For example, the pressure and desire to conform have been significant factors in the rapid proliferation of the cell phone and smartphone. When my friend purchased a camera phone several years back, it was still novel enough for people to give it a second glance. Now, even elementary school students carry smartphones.

The Korean cell phone industry has profited and developed thanks to Koreans' need to conform. Those who refuse the latest hairstyle or insist on old-fashioned health care products may find Korea unwelcoming. But those who walk to a different beat from the ant army will be rewarded with their own private beach or hiking trail.

 **Q** *Rotating red, white, and blue poles?*

What do those thin, vertical red, white and blue rotating poles (quite often in pairs) with an orange lamp on top signify?

—Chasing Rainbows

 **A** It's the sign for a barber shop. But in Korea, you may want to be careful. Many barber shops in entertainment districts often provide some special, er, massage services after the haircut—which can be declined. The more "services" you get, the more you pay, of course.

You enjoy such services at your own risk—be aware that you can get arrested for illegal activities. How do you tell which shops provide more than just a haircut? It's easy. The dodgy ones have twin signs and are mostly located downtown. Many of them also have a little post that reads (in Korean) "credit card welcome." These days, some massage parlors and so-called *hyugetel*, or male-only "rest hotels," have adopted the same signs, sparking strong protests from the nation's barbershop association, which claims the signs should be used by their establishments only.

A HAIRY QUESTION: KOREA'S BARBERSHOPS AND BEAUTY SALONS

BY ROBERT KOEHLER

Korea can be a mighty intimidating place for expats to get their hair cut. Aside from the obvious linguistic issues, Korea is blessed with a multiplicity of places to alter your coiffure. Deciding which one is right for you can be confusing—some serve both men and women, some serve men only, and others serve men more than just one type of blow-dry.

There wasn't always such a plethora of places in Korea to get your hair cut. In fact, for much of Korea's long and illustrious history, Buddhist monks were just about the only Koreans who regularly cut their hair. "Every part of your body is from your parents," it was taught, "so doing no harm to it is filial piety." Because of this Confucian precept, Koreans used to grow their hair long. Men tied their hair in a topknot and covered it with a hat; women tied theirs in a bun and kept it in place with a hairpin.

This changed after Japan's victory in the Sino-Japanese War, when reformist Prime Minister Kim Hong-jip issued a November 1895 decree calling on men to cut off their topknots. King Gojong set an example by being the first to chop his hair short, while Kim ordered officials onto the streets with scissors to give forced haircuts to anyone seen sporting long hair. In 1901, Korea's first barbershop—the Dongheung Barbershop—was set up in Insa-dong. Women would have to wait a little longer, until 1933, when Oh Yeop-ju—fresh from completing cosmetology studies in Japan—returned to found Korea's first beauty salon, the Hwashin Beauty Salon, in the old Hwashin Department Store on Jongno Road.

Nowadays, Koreans generally make use of barbershops, beauty salons, and public bathhouses to get their hair cut and styled. Barbershops were once important social institutions, staffed by male barbers and frequented by male clients. Such establishments could be found on almost every city street and in every small town. Nowadays, however, the institution is viewed as an endangered species thanks to the proliferation of essentially unisex beauty salons.

Barbershops generally come in two flavors—*ibalso* and *iyongwon*. An *ibalso* is, more often than not, a legitimate hair cutting establishment. Male clients go to get their hair cut by a trained male barber for about 10,000 won. It's also a good place to get a shave. Barbers tend to be traditionalists, as are the bulk of their (overwhelmingly middle-aged) clients, so if you're looking for one of those crazy David Beckham cuts, steer clear of the *ibalso*.

The *iyongwon*, on the other hand, is often staffed with a male barber and female masseuses. Like its *ibalso* cousin, its clientele is entirely male, although usually financially better off. At a legitimate *iyongwon*, you can get a cut, a shave, and a decent massage for something like 60,000–80,000 won. At many such establishments, however, the masseuses are more than just masseuses. This extra "service" is illegal but fairly widespread in Korea, despite intensifying efforts on the part of the authorities to crack down on it. As for how to differentiate between the legitimate barbershops and the dodgy ones, it's anyone's guess, but if you enter an establishment and are greeted by a woman wearing lingerie, chances are you've arrived at a place specializing in services other than haircuts.

The beauty salon (*miyongsil*) began life as a female-only establishment—the hairdressers were women, as were its clientele. They used to specialize in perms and hair colorings, but nowadays they also cut hair using both scissors and clippers (a source of friction with the

Korea Barbershop Society). And with more men demanding more daring hairstyles than can be obtained at the barbershop, beauty salons are frequented by increasing numbers of male clients, especially younger ones. Korea has even witnessed the rise of Blue Club, an economy beauty salon chain specializing in men's hair design.

Then there is the public bathhouse. The men's section of most public bathhouses in Korea usually has its own in-house barbers who cut the hair of clients for prices similar to those you might find at a beauty salon. It goes without saying that bathhouse barbers do not usually offer shampoos and shaves. This is a favored option for many Korean men who find it a pain to visit a specialized establishment—a barbershop or beauty salon, for instance—to get a simple haircut.

BARBERSHOP

5 SHOPPER'S DELIGHT

The moment that all the women (and even the men) have
been waiting for: shopping!

First things first. The Korean Dude shall dispel any
fantastic misconceptions you may have about shopping in Korea.
If you are expecting to buy cheap products, consider yourself
warned. Prices of consumer goods have been increasing and will
continue to do so—one downside of rapid economic progress, to
say the least. Thanks to a culture obsessed with consumerism,
however, you will find that the variety of products and services is
vast and profuse in the megacity that is Seoul. From traditional
markets to major retail, antique, and electronic districts, Seoul
has something for all ages and sexes.

While most stores go by the price tag, there's still some wiggle
room for those ever-elusive unbelievable deals. With the right sort
of retail insight, you should be able to find some of them hiding
just within your reach.

Q *What sort of retail is available in Korea?*

—Shopaholic

Koreans love to shop. Large Korean cities are full of shopping opportunities, ranging from bustling food markets to monumentally expensive designer goods outlets and department stores. The greatest variety is available in Seoul, where the huge Dongdaemun and Namdaemun markets draw a steady torrent of shoppers in search of clothes, food, household items, and street food, as well as sheer atmosphere. The capital's department stores and boutiques service those in search of high fashion, while gadget enthusiasts also find what they are looking for in locales like the electronics malls of Yongsan.

What goods are worth purchasing in Korea (in terms of competitive prices) depends on which country you're coming from. Japanese tourists, for example, often buy dried seaweed (*gim*), glasses, and medical services. Some electronic goods, including digital cameras, may be cheaper in Korea than in European countries.

Price differences aside, there are plenty of unique Korean goods worth taking back to your home country. Traditional products include ceramics, ginseng, tea, traditional paper

goods, fabrics (such as naturally dyed hemp and ramie), and paintings. Folk art and craft like traditional Korean clothing (*hanbok*), fans, wooden masks, embroidery, painted ducks (as wedding gifts, they symbolize life-long fidelity), kites, mother-of-pearl inlaid lacquerware, and ceramics are also popular at shopping locales like Seoul's Insa-dong. Some of these products can be bought for just a few thousand won; others, including items made by master craftsmen, are works of art that cost hundreds of thousands of won.

Other popular purchases in Korea include clothing, sportswear, leather and fur goods, antiques and replicas, jewelry, traditional liquor, and foodstuffs.

Q Is haggling common in the marketplace?

I have been studying Korean for four years. Our textbooks teach us about haggling at open-air markets. But when I have tried this in Seoul, following all the instructions and vocabulary outlined in our texts, I have gotten nowhere. I smile, offer 30 percent below the asking price, make sure to always use

jondaemal (honorifics or respectful language in Korea), try walking away—it never works. Should we not even try? Is haggling for Koreans only?

—Empty-Walleted

The Dude guesses you failed because you suggested a very high discount. There was once a time—perhaps very long ago—when the fixed-price system was rarely observed by Korean shop owners. These days, however, most shops are adopting fixed prices—even mom-and-pop establishments and stores located within traditional open markets like Dongdaemun and Namdaemun. Moreover, changes in Korean society mean you no longer expect peddlers at famous tourist attractions to rip off foreigners.

So a discount of five to ten percent usually works well for the Dude when he goes to the market. Some of his more gifted friends may manage 20 to 30 percent discount—arriving armed with knowledge about appropriate prices, skills of persuasion, and the ability to read minds. Meanwhile, foreign shoppers not only are hamstrung by the language different but also miss all the nonverbal cues of the merchants. The Dude still recommends you suggest a small discount before making the decision to purchase by saying *Jogeumman kkakkajuseyo?* ("Would you please give me a little discount?") and hovering around an item for some time.

Haggling is not essential at Korean markets, and many retailers simply refuse to haggle. But every situation is different, and sometimes discounts can be squeezed out. Do remember that most of the time, prices have not been overinflated in the anticipation of bargaining.

Q *Is it easy to find genuine antiques in Korea?*

How can I know if they're genuine? And if they are, am I allowed to take them out of the country?

—Treasure Hunter

A Most antique hunters in Seoul head for Insa-dong, where small shops often hold treasure troves of old objects. Perhaps the easiest way to reach Insa-dong is to take subway Line 3 to Anguk Station. Other areas in Seoul with clusters of antique shops are Itaewon (Line 6) and Dapsimni (Line 5). It always helps to have a Korean speaker along with you, especially when hunting for antiques outside of Seoul.

It's not always easy for non-experts to be sure whether an antique is genuine or real. But it is forbidden by law to leave Korea with items that are more than 50 years old and have been judged to hold value as cultural properties. It may be a good idea to have your antiques appraised at an office of Cultural Properties Appraisal (available at all seaports and airports in Korea) to confirm their age, authenticity, and cultural value. The Korean Antiques Association (02-732-2240) near Anguk Station offers an expert appraisal service for objects that may or may not be antiques, although this is not available in English.

If you are apprehensive about actually purchasing antiques and simply want to view them, there are several museums where you can do so, including the Korea Furniture Museum in Seoul; Kojeon Antique in Yongin; and the Hanul Theme Museum in Yeoju-gun, Gyeonggi-do.

ELECTRONICS SHOPPER'S PARADISE:
HOW AND WHERE TO SHOP

BY JOEL BROWNING

As the base of major electronics and microprocessor corporations like LG and Samsung, and home to the Yongsan Electronics Market, one of the largest of its kind in the world, Seoul is a great place to find and buy high-quality electronics at reasonable prices. It is also a big city, however, and the purchasing of electronics can sometimes seem complex to the inexperienced.

Prepare, Prepare, Prepare

One of the most common mistakes consumers make is going to a store with only a vague notion of what they want, and no idea of how much it costs. This can result in them being led blindly by the salesperson and purchasing more than they need at an inflated cost. By reading product reviews, comparing prices with foreign electronics marts like Bestbuy or Amazon, and taking the extra time to figure out what the model specifications mean, consumers can arm themselves with the necessary knowledge to meet salespeople on an equal footing. A little information goes a long way in the tech world. Get informed on the specifics of computer hardware components like RAM and processors, and research whether the MP3 player requires third party software or uses flash memory. The specifics of these components are what allow consumers to pick a model tailored to their individual needs.

Making the Buy

After you choose your model, the next step is deciding where to make your purchase. There are three basic options for purchasing electronics.

The first of these options is the Internet. Korea is one of the most wired societies in the world, and its online shopping has developed proportionally. Traditionally, bartering at markets was the cheapest way to procure electronic goods. But with the advent of the Internet, products are now that much cheaper.

The Internet does have its drawbacks, however. For those who prefer the hands-on aspect of shopping and the instantaneous reward of the purchase, hitting up one of the other two options, electronic markets and electronics stores, remains the best choice. Electronics markets can be found in a variety of places throughout Seoul, but the most prominent among them is the Yongsan Electronics Market. It's home to an estimated 5,000 separate electronics shops.

Because of the sheer number of retailers in such close proximity, Yongsan truly is a buyers' market. As a result, haggling is perfectly acceptable, and often encouraged. Shops sell nearly identical items, and the only way to stay in business amid such extreme competition is by clinching the sale. Putting in legwork is one of the most underappreciated aspects of haggling. Merely by walking around from shop to shop and comparing prices, you'll receive a variety of offers from salespeople trying to nab the sale. This, coupled with a little creative bargaining, can result in a price significantly discounted from those of chain or department stores, and accessories and extras that shop owners often receive free from vendors further sweeten the pot.

Buyer Beware

Yongsan also has its downside. Korea, while currently in the process of opening its market through a variety of FTAs with the US and EU, still has a high level of restrictions on imported goods. As a result, domestic electronics, especially Korean computer parts and digital cameras, are among the best deals, while imported electronics like Sony or Apple are more expensive. Also, because competition is so fierce, shops will often go out of business. This poses problems, especially in the case of computer systems, when the warranty for the product is not a manufacturer warranty. Customers must collect as much information as possible from the salesperson and shop owner to protect their investment for the full length of their warranty. In this case, purchases at chain or department stores will cost the consumer more, but provide peace of mind in the end.

WHITHER THE KOREAN MARKET?
Future of traditional markets uncertain

BY ANNE HILTY

In Korea, there is a delicate balance between old and new, traditional and modern. Some fear that traditions are being lost; others worry that Korea isn't yet modern enough to compete on a global level. One of the most obvious examples of this conflict can be seen in the markets.

There are supermarkets throughout Seoul—NH Hanaro Mart, Grand Mart, and GS Supermarket—as well as the hypermarkets E-mart, Costco, Lotte Mart, and HomePlus, to name a few. Whether a department store, large discount chain, or supermarket, modern markets abound, offering the latest items, as well as many foreign ones. Convenience stores can be found on every corner, representing a smaller version of the modern market.

These have become the new rivals of traditional markets, such as those located near Sindang-dong, Yeongdeungpo, Sangil-dong, Moran-dong, Garak-dong, Nonhyeon-dong, Cheongdam-dong, Yeoksam-dong, or Bupyeong. These (typically outdoor) markets offer everything from food and clothes to household goods, and even livestock. There are numerous specialty markets both traditional and modern, such as Noryangjin for fish, Dongdaemun for discount apparel, and Myeong-dong or Apgujeong for high fashion, as well as the Art Freemarket at Hongdae area, Gyeong-dong for herbal medicine, Yongsan for electronics, Yeji-dong for jewelry,

Janganpyeong for antiques, Yangjae for flowers, Chungmuro for livestock and pets, and Insa-dong for cultural artifacts and souvenirs. Add to that ethnic markets that serve the small Filipino, Russian, Japanese, Chinese, French, and Mongolian communities, among others, in various corners of the city.

Traditional markets recall a bazaar in the Middle East—or a flea market in the West. Hundreds, sometimes thousands, of vendors (such as those in Namdaemun, Noryangjin, or Gyeong-dong) sell their wares at the market. The booths, tables, and tiny shops are crowded together, presenting a microcosm of many Asian cities; the sounds, sights, and scents mix into a tapestry that swirls around the shoppers, placing each of them well within the story that it has to tell. It is an immersion experience, and one of the best ways for a foreigner to get a sense of Korean culture.

The Seoul Metropolitan Government reports the existence of 312 traditional markets, including 112 that aren't officially registered and simply spring up from time to time in various locations. The Seoul Development Institute classifies them as small neighborhood, medium specialized, and large-scale markets; more than half are over 20 years old. But foreign distributors (permitted since 1996) have exponentially heated up the battle between modern and conventional.

Other competitors of the traditional market are online and television-based shopping, both of which are swiftly gaining popularity. Attempts by traditional markets to modernize, such as an Internet site representing Namdaemun Market vendors, have been largely unsuccessful: only one-tenth of the vendors at Namdaemun Market participate in the online site. Many would argue that attempts to modernize traditional markets will change them forever, making them into something that they're not—the same hybrid of old and new that's reflected in so many other attempts at cultural preservation. Others rightly stress that modernization is, at this point, a matter of survival as the number of buyers at the conventional markets continues to decline.

Much discussion is taking place over the future of Seoul's traditional markets, as witnessed in various newspapers, magazine articles, and Internet sites. As Seoulites become increasingly modern and globally connected, they are rejecting the traditional markets more and more. There is also a generational factor, in that young people typically embrace all things modern while their elders attempt to hold on to tradition. While trends can be identified, the future of conventional markets is far from certain as Korea tries to protect its traditions and culture from further erosion. Never is the struggle between modernity and tradition more apparent than in the marketplace of Seoul.

6 FOR THE VAGABONDS

Like travelers everywhere, tourists in Korea will have certain questions about what to expect. After all, who doesn't want to make sure that they're not going to die while out and about in a foreign country?

While South Korea certainly does not rank among the more difficult countries to traverse, there are some aspects of travel that you may wish to familiarize yourself with before attempting to become the next great explorer of the world. For example, how do you ensure that you will have a place to sleep at night? Not to mention that figuring out what safety precautions to take before visiting would be a smart idea, wouldn't it?

As safe and neon-lit a country as Korea may be, it's never fun to be stuck solo in the dead of night, especially in unfamiliar terrain. Read on to arm yourself with some additional tourism *savoir faire.*

Q *Is it easy to travel in Korea without being able to speak the language?*

—Monoglot

The numerous signs in English and the decent knowledge of English exhibited by many Korean citizens—all augmented by excellent public transportation and numerous tourist-oriented organizations—can make travel in Korea both easy and overwhelming.

Major tourist areas, such as those in Seoul, tend to be signposted in English; areas like Insa-dong, Samcheong-dong, and Itaewon offer tourist information booths to help travelers get around. Almost all road signs and signposts at railway stations and major bus terminals are written in both Korean and English. Subway trains and buses also announce upcoming stops in several languages. Because the public transportation systems are set up so efficiently and include detailed maps of the area around the stations, you don't often require much more to make your way around.

Most public employees are expected to possess a certain level of competency in the English language, so ticket purchasing and similar activities should not be terribly difficult. Likewise, many retail venues also require their employees to speak foreign languages, particularly in high-profile tourist shopping areas such as Itaewon and Myeong-dong in Seoul. Incidentally, many venues in such areas also accept certain types of foreign currency, reducing the need for currency exchange at the bank.

For times when on-the-spot interpretation is absolutely necessary, Korea Travel Phone (dial 1330 with the local area code) is a telephone service that provides comprehensive English-language information for tourists. Taxis have their own interpretation services as well, which should be posted in the vehicles. Even 119, Korea's emergency number, offers interpretation services, as do several other public services. Be warned, however, that many of these numbers begin their services in Korean—not a very smart decision on the part of operators.

It is also quite common for people traveling in Korea's cities and provinces to encounter friendly locals who speak varying degrees of English and go out of their way to help visitors get around. In short, while you may not be able to converse with all the Koreans you meet, language should not pose a serious obstacle to traveling in this beautiful country.

TRANSLATION AND INTERPRETATION SERVICES

- **BBB Volunteer Service for Translation:** To access a volunteer translator, dial (02) 1588-5644 and follow the prompt for your language.

- **1330 Travel Phone Emergency Interpretation Service (land line):** 1330

  By mobile phone: Area code + 1330 (e.g., 02-1330 in Seoul)
  (Service charge: Charged as local call)

  Calling from abroad: 82-(area code*)-1330
  (e.g., +82-2-1330 in Seoul)
  *Be sure to drop the first 0 in the area code.

Q *Is Korea a safe destination for single female travelers?*

—Miss Daredevil

Korea is very safe to travel by global standards, and this applies to single female travelers, too. But it wouldn't hurt to take caution of the things you would in any other country or city.

- When riding a cab late at night, call for a taxi (International Taxi, T. 1644-2255), instead of catching one passing by

- Take good care of your personal belongings when in a crowd. I would recommend you to carry your bag in front of you when on a subway or bus.
- Don't walk alone in deserted/dark areas, especially when it's late.
- Stay with the crowd, with women, if possible.

Q *What is the policy regarding weapons?*

—Trigger Happy

Korea has strict laws on firearms ownership, and getting permission for firearm-related activities can be very difficult. In fact, guns are generally used and carried only by military personnel and police, although police officers more commonly use alternative weapons such as batons.

In principle, the law prohibits all civilians from possessing, selling, and carrying firearms. Limited exceptions are made for sporting shooters (as certified by the Korea Shooting Federation) and professional hunters, although the proper authorities must always be notified whenever firearms are being used and/or transported. Citizens approved for firearm possession are required to renew their permits every five years.

Thanks to such strict regulations, gun-related crime and death rates are very, very low in Korea.

Q Is accommodation expensive or difficult to find?

What accommodation options are available?

—Sleepy

A wide range of accommodation is available throughout Korea. From super-deluxe hotels to dormitory beds in youth hostels, there are price and convenience options to suit every traveler. Interesting options include temple stays, which usually involve one or two nights at one of Korea's beautiful Buddhist temples, and traditional *hanok* accommodations. Both are ways of combining a night's sleep with the experience of Korean traditional culture.

Business travelers staying for several weeks or months can make use of residential suites or serviced residences. Still another option is to stay at a luxury country resort with spa, golf, or other facilities. Korea Tourism Organization also has a "Goodstay" designation system to help travelers choose from among the country's thousands of cheap motels (http://www.goodstay.or.kr). A night at a good motel is surprisingly good value for your money—some rooms that are not too different from those of a more expensive hotel are available for as little as 50,000 won.

7 NAVIGATION

As much as the Korean Dude has indicated that Korea is not a hugely difficult country to navigate, many travelers—particularly those used to the clearly named and marked roads and streets of the West—may find the absence of street signs in Korea somewhat disorienting. One may also notice that the city of Seoul is not designed as a grid, but with circular infrastructure. This means that expanding the city's boundaries is exceedingly difficult, and that, in turn, means that any alterations to the city generally happen within its borders. Result: more chaos!

But never fear: there is a trick to making your way in Korea. Yes, the country is constantly changing. Certainly, whatever signage there is becomes obsolete quickly—which is one reason Koreans don't rely on such resources. But a little quick thinking and a lot of common sense should be enough to get you around.

The following are testimonials from fellow foreigners who have been faced with difficulties in navigating Korea. Hopefully, their insights will help you in mapping out your own adventure.

Q

How do you find your way around, especially if there are no street signs?

—A-maze-ingly Lost

A

Major tourist areas tend to be signposted in English, but those signs are generally not used in the context of giving directions. The easiest way to get around in Seoul, like other cities with subway systems, is to familiarize yourself with the local subway system and the areas outside of it. Subway maps are a good way to learn about the general layout of cities; in Seoul, there are stations for just about every neighborhood. One easy way to plan ahead is to find out the nearest station exit to your destination and look at the map to note major landmarks along the way.

If you ever get lost, rest assured that there is usually a subway station somewhere nearby. If regaining your sense of direction seems well nigh impossible, you can always use taxis, which are cheap and plentiful in Korea. One option for visitors traveling via rental car is to use a navigation system. These nifty devices not only help direct you where to go, but also provide speeders with real-time notifications of where speed cameras are located!

Ms. Expat Says...

LOST IN SEOUL

BY NANCY KIM

Giving directions in Seoul is no easy feat. Neighborhoods are clusters of spidery alleys, feared by even the most seasoned of taxi drivers. Streets have names, but for the most part they go unused or unknown by the general public. Addresses, with their cryptic combination of numbers, "*dong*"s, "*ga*"s, and "*ro*"s, are left to be deciphered only by postal workers and Chinese food delivery guys.

Perhaps this is why people tend to pick out some easy-to-find coffee shop, fast food restaurant, or subway station exit, meeting up there and proceeding to the final destination together. When I first came to Korea, the place to meet in Sinchon was in front of Yonsei Yak-guk (pharmacy). But that pharmacy changed ownership and was renamed "Daehan Yak-guk." The new name caused confusion, and the meeting place of choice was changed to the front entrance of the (very prominent) Hyundai Department Store. This seemed to be a good move, given the large plaza in front of the store, as opposed to the tiny sidewalk in front of the pharmacy. But on any given weekend evening, there will be hordes of people standing in front of the department store, and not because of the great sales and giveaway promotions.

Ironically, so many people use this as their meeting place that finding the person you are meeting is now as hard as finding a restaurant in Korea that doesn't serve pickles with spaghetti. It's possible, but it'll take you a while. A few months ago, I invited a friend who had just moved to Korea to come out and join me and my friends in Hongdae (the area around Hongik University). I tried to explain where we were using easy-to-follow directions. I couldn't tell him the names of most of the places because he couldn't read Korean, so I described all the surrounding restaurants and nightclubs.

I never realized until then how similar all the places looked. "There's a restaurant where everyone is grilling meat on old drum cans," I said. "Oh. Then there's another restaurant where everyone is grilling meat on old drum cans." About 15 minutes, later he called and asked if I was anywhere near the smokestacks. "Smokestacks? There aren't any smokestacks in Hongdae area." Maybe this is the reason most Koreans swarm like bees in front of department stores and fast food joints.

A few weeks later, I was meeting the same friend at the Mapo subway station. To eliminate any possibility of a repeat of the Hongdae area smokestack fiasco, we were to meet in front of Hana Bank, just a little walk from Exit 2. When he called to say he couldn't find the bank, I started to worry.

"Did you pass the construction site?"

"Yes."

"What about the post office?"

"Yes."

"What about the convenience store?"

"Yes, I passed that, too."

"But Hana Bank is right next to the convenience store. There's a big sign. You should be able to see it!"

"I can't see the bank, but I can see the World Cup Stadium," Jason offered helpfully.

I knew that was impossible, so I patronizingly asked him if he wasn't looking at a picture of the World Cup Stadium.

"I know the difference between a picture and a real building, Nancy."

There was a slight hint of irritation in his voice. It was only when he asked a passerby where the Holiday Inn Hotel was that we realized he hadn't gotten off at Mapo Station, but at Mapo-gu Office Station—where, the World Cup Stadium is, indeed, in full view.

What are the chances that two sections of the city could have a construction site, a post office, and a convenience store in quick succession? In Seoul, greater than zero. (Other confusing subway stops to look out for include Sinchon/Sincheon, Omokgyo/Mokdong, and Express Bus Terminal/Nambu Bus Terminal.) Lessons learned from these experiences? Always ask to meet at the nearest Starbucks. There's one everywhere, and if either party gets lost somewhere in the alleyways and underground passages of Seoul, at least the other can sit back and wait with a caramel macchiato.

BUS TRANSPORTATION:
HOW TO MAKE SENSE OF THE MAZE

BY YOUNGHI SEO

As far as public transportation is concerned, Seoul has a very efficient subway system. If you're used to riding the underground in other big cities, it's not too difficult to navigate and get around. What most foreigners don't know, though, is how efficient the bus transportation system is in Seoul. There is virtually no place that a bus won't go. And despite the frequent bottlenecks (any hour could be rush hour in this *ppalli ppalli* culture!), sometimes a bus will take you to your destination quicker than the subway.

For one thing, buses often offer more direct routes. If you don't speak or read Korean, it can be daunting to try getting around Seoul by bus. Never mind the hazards of traffic conditions and driving practices—the city seems vast, and really foreign even to some Koreans. But, as one friend pointed out when I first arrived in Seoul ten years ago, how am I going to get to know the city if I stay underground all the time?

I knew the language, but I was still afraid of getting lost. My friend, who is American, offered me some good advice: take advantage of the bus system. If a bus is going in the general direction I need to go, I should get on (and hold on)! Then, if I get lost, I can always hop in a taxi for the rest of the way to my destination. Considering that fares are relatively cheap in Seoul compared to other cities, what did I have to lose? Needless to say, I got lost a few times. But I also got to know the city pretty well.

Buses were first introduced as public transportation in Seoul in April 1928. Since then, the government has built many roads and added bus routes as an urban planning effort to deal with its fast-growing population. In July 2004, Seoul Metropolitan Government launched a new and more efficient bus system, which incorporated the needs of a growing international community. The new system adjusted all of the old bus routes and their numbers.

City buses are now organized into colors: green, blue, red, and yellow buses. Green buses connect between major subway stations or bus stops in downtown Seoul. Blue buses connect suburban areas to downtown Seoul. These have access to the new median bus-only lanes, which makes traveling faster than before. Red buses (express buses) are for connecting the outer metropolitan areas, like Bundang and Ilsan, to downtown Seoul.

Yellow buses circle around downtown Seoul and are particularly good for access to major shopping areas and businesses.

In addition, each city sector (*gu* in Korean) operates smaller buses, known as *maeul* (village) buses, which run from most major subway stations into local neighborhoods.

To complement the new bus system and make it easier to access, the Seoul Metropolitan Government also launched an English-language online bus route search system for Seoul's international community in December 2004. The Seoul Map shows detailed maps of local roads with the locations of major public institutions, buildings, schools, and hospitals, while the Bus Map shows bus routes and connecting subway stations. The user-friendly site is http://english.seoul.go.kr.

Finally, a new transfer card system was introduced in conjunction with the new bus transportation system to make city traveling easier. Known as "T-money," the cards can be picked up for 2,500 won at any subway station and some convenience stores. They are rechargeable, so you don't have to carry loose change around. The basic fare with the card is 1,050 won, or 100 won less than if you used currency (1,150 won). The biggest advantage, however, is that you can transfer for free from bus to bus or from bus to subway up to five times, as long as you do so within 30 minutes (or one hour after 9 p.m.). The system makes using the public transportation in the city very affordable! The only thing is, you have to remember to touch the card to the reader when you exit the bus, and not just when you get on. If you don't, you may be charged double the next time you use the card to get around!

So hop on a bus and have an aboveground adventure in Seoul!

EATS &
DRINKS

1 THE FAST TRACK TO FOOD COMA

Finally, the section that most of you have probably been starving for: food! Needless to say, Korea, like most other ethnic cultures of the world, has a diverse array of cuisine and tastes that present a unique take on this culture. To add to Korea's epicurean rapport, Korean food is also reputedly one of the healthiest ethnic cuisines in the world. Take that, foreigners who think *galbi* and *bulgogi* are the only defining Korean dishes!

Let's start with some basic table manners. While you will read more about the story behind these practices later in the "Culture Shock" chapter, do take note of these things not to do at the dinner table:

- Don't cross your utensils at mealtimes.

- When sitting down for a meal, younger diners should not take up their chopsticks or begin eating before their elders have done so.

- Chopsticks should not be planted upright in a bowl of rice or other food. They should always be laid down next to the bowl or plate.

- When pouring or receiving glasses of an alcoholic beverage, you should always use two hands in front of somebody of senior status. When drinking from a glass poured by somebody senior, you should turn your upper body to the side, indicating respect.

- It is considered impolite to whistle or sing at the table.

- Koreans in their 30s or older do not usually go Dutch when eating or drinking together. Common practice is for one person to pay the bill, and that person is usually the most senior person present—although the custom is now shifting toward taking turns at paying.

 *Why no talking at the dinner table?*

Why do some Korean people eat their meals without having any conversation? It seems to be the older generation that does this the most. At least for me, this results in a hugely awkward and uncomfortable eating experience, which is only made worse by the fact that, since people in Korea never eat alone, I can't exactly dine *sans* company. This continues to be one of the most puzzling customs I have witnessed.

—Missing Communication

There is a Korean proverb that goes, "If you speak while eating, fortune will avoid you." The proverb has something to do with Confucian tradition, in which juniors have to be cautious about keeping food inside the mouth when dining with their seniors. In the same context, they should chew food with their mouths shut. But being speechless is not confined only to dining. Another proverb says, "Those who speak much will perish by

their own words." If you aren't talking much, then another Korean expression: applies: "Your mouth is heavy." A "heavy mouth" is regarded as good, but a "light mouth" (i.e., someone who gossips and chatters often) is not.

Rest assured, dinnertime silence is fading as the norm for table customs, except perhaps in company outings. During such occasions, the person who pays the bill (usually the senior of the group) talks for the majority of the time. And even this has been changing recently, as company outings grow considerably more casual with the conversation.

 But who cares about manners when there's food? If you're like the Dude and overwhelmed easily by an overabundance of epicurean choice, the following will give you a good idea of where to start. First, we'll start with the big staple:

Q *What is the origin of kimchi?*

As I've been living in Korea for some time now, I have grown quite accustomed to the Korean staple food kimchi in all its flavors and variations. I've heard rumors that kimchi is, in fact, of Chinese origin, not Korean. This seems strange, as I've been to China twice, and I've never seen kimchi or anything like it being served to customers. So is kimchi originally from Korea or China, or from somewhere else entirely? Do people in other countries eat it in the same volume and manner that they do in Korea?

—Seasoned to Kimchi

 In the past, there were some kinds of kimchi in China—a Chinese book from the 6th century mentioned various ways to store vegetables using salt and fermentation. As for Korea, it's assumed that kimchi was eaten as early as the Three Kingdoms Period (roughly 18 BC–AD 660), judging from the excavation of large earthen jars and written records of salted seafood at the time.

The first records of focused kimchi study appear in the *Dongguk Isanggukjip*, a collection of writings by Yi Gyu-bo in the early 13th century. "Radish tastes good in summer if preserved in soybean paste, and lasts throughout the winter if preserved in salt," the book explains. Not only radish but also cabbage might have been used for kimchi now that another book from that period mentioned the existence of cabbage.

But one ingredient was missing from kimchi at that time: red pepper. That spice was introduced to Korea during the Hideyoshi invasion of 1592 to 1598—not as a food, but as a weapon. It took red pepper about 200 years to find its rightful place in kimchi, according to a 1766 book titled *Jeungbo Salim Gyeongje (Revised Forestry Economy)*.

In conclusion: yes, like many other things in Korea, kimchi does combine a number of foreign goods. It also illustrates a typical take on the relationship between Korea and fermentation culture: everything is fermented when it arrives at this peninsula. Ultimately, you could say that kimchi is the tasty outcome of a creative experiment.

SAY KIMCHI!:
EVERYTHING YOU WANTED TO KNOW ABOUT KOREA'S NATIONAL DISH BUT WERE AFRAID TO ASK

BY YOUNGHI SEO

If you've ever walked by a group of Korean tourists getting their pictures taken, you've probably heard them yelling "kimchi!" as they stand in front of the camera. Although it may seem odd to foreigners that they are yelling the name of a side dish, this is actually the same as saying "cheese!" in English.

In Korea, kimchi is the most common side dish, one that you will find at almost every meal. This traditional Korean dish is made of pickled and fermented vegetables, usually Chinese cabbage (called *baechu*) mixed with garlic, salt, vinegar, chili peppers, and other spices.

November is a special month for kimchi, as it is traditionally known as the month for *gimjang*, or kimchi-making. This is an annual Korean event where a large amount of kimchi is prepared for *Umdong*, the coldest months of winter. *Gimjang* starts in late October or early November and usually lasts for two to three days. Traditionally, many people would gather in a house during *gimjang* season to help the hostess make kimchi for that household. Since each household usually prepared about 100 to 200 cabbages, relatives and neighbors would get together to help the family. Once they finished making kimchi for one family, they helped the next household with their *gimjang*. In this way, everyone finished their kimchi-making by helping one another.

Although *baechu* kimchi is the most common kind today, this is actually a relatively recent development. The history of kimchi dates back as far as the seventh century when kimchi was born as a kind of pickled vegetable. Although at first kimchi was just a form of salted vegetable, during the 12th century some spices and seasonings were added. Later in the 18th century, hot red pepper became one of the major spices for kimchi when it was introduced by Portuguese traders coming from Japan in the 16th century. Therefore, it was only during the late Joseon era that kimchi became associated with its vibrant red color.

Finally, the well-known *baechu* kimchi was made after the introduction of Chinese cabbage in the 19th century. Although this is now the most famous variety, the Kimchi Field Museum in Seoul has documented up to 187 total varieties of the side dish. The variants are made with radish, garlic stalks, eggplant, and mustard leaf, among other ingredients.

Kimchi is also well known for its nutritional attributes. *The American Health Magazine* cited kimchi as one of world's five "healthiest foods," noting that it is loaded with vitamins A, B, and C. The so-called "healthy bacterium" lactobacillus, which is found in fermented kimchi, helps with digestion, and even prevents yeast infections. The fermented cabbage of kimchi also contains compounds that may prevent the growth of cancer. With all these great properties, no wonder Koreans were so eager to take this dish to the final frontier, developing "space kimchi" for Korea's first astronaut, Yi So-yeon, to take with her on her April 2008 journey. Incidentally, many space crews like spicy food, not least because the fluid shifting to the head in orbit reduces your sense of taste. Kimchi has also been found to be effective in treating fowl infected with the bird flu virus. LG Electronics has developed air conditioners, nicknamed "Anti-A.I. Aircon," that prevent avian influenza with a special filter coated in an anti-

bacterial substance extracted from fermented kimchi.

Despite all the benefits of kimchi, the *gimjang* tradition has been in decline, since the side dish can now be easily bought at any supermarket all year long. But you can still get a glimpse of this major Korean tradition through a kimchi festival like the Gwangju World Kimchi Culture Festival in October (http://kimchi.gwangju.go.kr). At such events, you can taste the different varieties of kimchi and take part in making it yourself free of charge.

If you want to learn more about kimchi but don't want to travel far from Seoul, you can still get tons of information at the Kimchi Field Museum. The museum is located at the COEX mall and is accessible from Exit 5 of Samsung Station, Line 2. The admission fee for adults is 3,000 won. For more information, call (02) 6002-6456 or visit the website at http://www. kimchimuseum.co.kr.

What are some moderately priced, readily accessible, healthy, low-calorie, filling, and tasty local dishes?

Korean food is supposed to be so healthy and nutritious, but since arriving here five years ago, I have gained roughly 20 kilograms primarily sticking to a Korean diet. I don't exercise much at all, but I didn't before I came here, either. Could you recommend some moderately priced, readily accessible, healthy, low-calorie, filling, and tasty local dishes (nothing with smelly fish heads or pig's feet, please) so I can start shedding some extra baggage and lose the love handles?

—Heavily Burdened

The formula for a healthy diet seems to be the same around the world; vegetables and grains are good for your diet. Luckily for you, authentic Korean food is considered to be one of the healthiest ethnic cuisines in the world, since it is made from all-natural ingredients. And most dishes are recognized for their tangible health benefits to boot. Here are some tips for healthy eating that you can follow even at many casual *sikdang* (Korean restaurants).

1) Instead of white rice, go with steamed rice mixed with black or yellow grains like unpolished rice, barley, and red beans, which have an abundance of fiber.

2) Try seaweeds like dried laver, brown seaweed, and kelp. Brown seaweed soup is so nutritious that Korean women usually eat it after giving birth to a baby, and it's also low in calories. Boiled kelp, which is good for constipation, is usually eaten with vinegared red pepper paste.

3) When you eat meat, try *bossam gogi* (boiled pork) rather than *samgyeopsal* (grilled pork) or *galbi-jjim* (marinated ribs). When it comes to chicken, *samgyetang* (ginseng chicken soup) is better than *dakdori-tang* (spicy chicken stew).

4) For a lot of vegetables, try dishes like *bibimbap* or *ssambap*.

5) Prepared through lactic fermentation, kimchi is known to be effective in stimulating the metabolism, reducing fat, and keeping you regular. There are non-spicy varieties out there, too, including *baekgimchi* (white kimchi).

6) Soybeans are well known for having enough protein to offset the decreased nutrient intake from fasting and light eating. Tofu (*dubu* in Korean) is also recognized as a good diet food. Of course, you should avoid fried tofu, since it absorbs a lot of oil. Instead, go with boiled or steamed preparations like *dubu jorim* (bean-curd stew) or *sundubu jjigae* (soft tofu soup). *Doenjang jjigae* (fermented soybean soup) is also recommended.

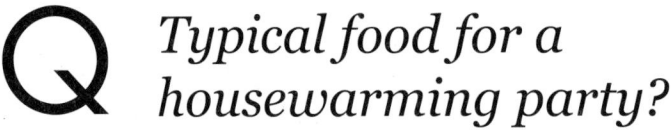

Q *Typical food for a housewarming party?*

What are the typical foods and drinks to prepare when inviting friends for a housewarming party in Korea? Apart from the de rigueur *soju*, what else is needed?

—Resident Cook

A *Galbi* and *samgyeopsal* are good, since they're relatively easy to prepare and suited to the housewarming atmosphere. Fruit and tea are typical for after the meal. Since you're a foreigner, however, some of your Korean friends might be expecting something exotic. It's quite all right to prepare your own dishes, explaining to your Korean friends about their cultural background. You'd be better off making some instant noodles or rice with kimchi for those unable to explore new foods, though. Generally speaking, Koreans are open to trying new food. The Dude should point out that the tradition of the housewarming party, or *jipdeuri*, is growing less common these days, so thank you for keeping the tradition alive.

SEOUL SURVIVOR:
BEATING THE HEAT OF KOREAN SUMMERS

BY NANCY KIM

As the mercury starts to rise throughout the land of morning calm, trepidation kicks in and Koreans nationwide begin to dread the inevitable hot and sticky summer. Their apprehension is often heightened by Korea Meteorological Administration predictions for a sweltering summer— terrible news for a country that must endure up to four months of temperatures peaking in the high 30s, plus humidity. But there are ways of beating the heat of Korea's scorching summers.

While hordes of vacationing Seoulites float along on the mass exodus to beaches dotting the peninsula's coast, I'm forced to seek relief closer to home. There are several summer fun options in the outdoors to choose from. Swimming and water sports can be found at the Hangang Park. Other destinations include the central business district, especially with the massive new Gwanghwamun Square. And down at City Hall, you can find kids frolicking in the fountains of Seoul Plaza in front of the complex.

In the end, however, I opt to go indoors. Step into any café or consumer business in Seoul and you're greeted with Arctic gusts from heavy duty A/C systems. Most store owners are aware that many of their summertime patrons are only feigning interest in the merchandise to enjoy the cool. If you're getting the evil eye, a movie ticket will get you a good 120 minutes of hassle-free bliss on the hottest summer days. Try a horror flick: the spine-chilling fright is sure to make your body temperature drop a bit more.

While A/C provides a great temporary relief from the smoldering heat outside, prolonged exposure to the frigid air may lead to hypothermia! A quick glance around any workplace where it's on full blast all day long will reveal that the employees are wrapped in sweaters and shawls—quite a contrast from the underdressed pedestrians outside the glass doors.

When it comes to eats, my choices are always icy, ranging from Korean *patbingsu* (consisting of some variety of shaved ice, sweetened red bean paste, fruit, and condensed milk) to the frozen fruit sticks sold out of street carts. However, traditionals may prefer a different kind of summer treat. The Korean saying of *i-yeol-chi-yeol* (translating roughly as "fight fire with fire") suggests that when you want to cool off in the summer, it's better to eat hot items instead of frostier fare. Such cuisine is referred to as *boyangsik*—hot, high-protein foods that are believed to re-energize the body, helping it recover from summertime lethargy and malaise. Korea's *boyangsik* cuisine is diverse (and includes one of Korea's most internationally controversial dishes). Here are the varieties:

Samgyetang (chicken ginseng soup)

Samgyetang is a dish of young chicken stuffed with glutinous rice, ginseng, garlic, Korean dates, and chestnuts and cooked in a bubbling hot broth. Its restorative properties are said to reenergize bodies during the draining summer. In addition, the hot broth will encourage perspiration, which helps, in turn, to cool off overheated diners.

When I first came to Korea, I didn't understand why my Korean friends would choose to torture themselves with a steaming bowl of chicken soup in the middle of summer. Watching them struggle over the *samgyetang*, faces beet red and dripping with sweat, was uncomfortable to say the least. I was always dumbfounded when they finished their meal with a comment about how "refreshing" it was. As doubtful as I was about this "fight fire with fire" idea, I did notice that my friends seemed to complain less about the heat after their *samgyetang* meal. You can usually score a dish for 11,000 to 15,000 won.

Otdak (chicken and lacquer sap soup)

Another summertime *boyangsik* favorite is *otdak*—chicken stewed in a broth of water with a touch of lacquer sap. The sap is said to be good for the liver and heart and particularly effective for beating summer lethargy. That said, you should be warned that it causes allergic skin rashes and itching in some people, something that should not surprise you given that the lacquer tree is closely related to poison ivy. *Otdak* usually costs around 40,000 won for four.

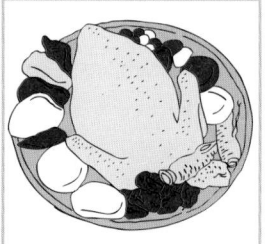

Jangeogui (broiled eel)

Jangeogui is particularly rich in vitamins A, B, and E, making it good for women's skin, fatigue prevention, and male stamina. To prepare the dish, cooks remove the bones from the eel, which is then brushed with a marinade of, among other things, sugar, garlic, and ginger. The meat is then broiled on a charcoal fire, providing diners with a rich and savory meal. Look to spend 15,000 won per person on this dish.

Chueotang (mudfish soup)

Chueotang is a soup that utilizes the entire mudfish—or, perhaps more accurately, the Chinese weatherfish, a hearty species that is found in muddy streams and rivers throughout Korea. The bones and innards of the fish are used, so the soup is rich in vitamins A and D, and especially in calcium. Its high protein count, coupled with its richness in the essential amino acid lysine, makes it particularly recommended for growing children and older people concerned about brittle bones. *Chueotang* is a spicy soup that uses a variety of greens. As you eat it, sweat will no doubt pour off your forehead. But as many peoples living in hot areas have learned—see, for instance, the traditional foods of the Arabian Peninsula—spicy foods have a curious way of making you feel cool. *Chueotang* might be one of the more cost-effective *boyangsik* options at 8,000 to 9,000 won a bowl.

Bosintang (dog meat soup)

Yes, some Koreans do eat dogs. As you are probably already aware, this is an area of domestic and international contention. Dog meat is technically illegal in Korea, although it more accurately falls into a legal gray area that hinders prosecution for its consumption. The effects of this are evident in the number of dog meat restaurants that operate very openly in Seoul, and you can be sure you will not be criminally charged with a dog meat-related offense. The slogan is that only dogs specially bred for human consumption are used for food, although many stories suggesting otherwise have been related in the media and other sources.

In the spirit of honest reporting, here is a breakdown of dog-based cuisine. The most representative dog meat dish is *bosintang*, a rich and spicy soup that also includes sesame leaves and other greens. The meat is often dipped in a sauce of mustard and sesame powder. Eating *bosintang* is still considered in some circles as something of a male-bonding experience, as it is usually men who will consume the dish. *Bosintang* and *samgyetang* were traditionally eaten in the shaded comfort of forested mountain streams and hillside pavilions on the *bongnal,* or the three days that mark the hottest stretch of the Korean summer—the "dog days," if you will. While you're unlikely to find Koreans in the streams and pavilions on *bongnal* nowadays unless they fall on a weekend, *samgyetang* and *bosintang* joints are usually pretty full. A bowl of *bosintang* will usually cost about 10,000 to 15,000 won.

I decided to try out the wisdom of my Korean friends and step into a *samgyetang* restaurant. As soon as I walked in, I was welcomed by another blast of cold air. Sigh. When will I ever learn? The key to surviving a Korean summer is to eat hot *samgyetang*—and always carry a sweater with you.

 *Why metal chopsticks?*

I hope you can provide me with the answer to a question that has been troubling me for a number of years now: Why are metal chopsticks the norm in Korea? In the course of my travels, I have found that Korea is alone in the widespread use of metal chopsticks. I have put the question to many Koreans over the past five years and received a diverse range of unsatisfactory answers. The only commonality was that the responders freely confessed to guessing and could not guarantee the correctness of their replies.

—Steel Wondering

The number of people who use chopsticks is estimated to be 1.6 billion in Korea, China, Japan, Singapore, Taiwan, Macau, and Vietnam alone, of which the first three Asian nations make up the lion's share with 80 percent. Whereas the Japanese use wooden chopsticks and the Chinese use bamboo or plastic ones, Koreans are perhaps the only ones to have such a widespread use of metal chopsticks among the general population. Many Koreans attribute the dexterity of the Korean people in areas such as arts, crafts, labor, and inventions to the use of metal chopsticks.

The practice appears to date back to at least the 6th century AD, when metal chopsticks were included among the objects left in the tomb of King Muryeong of Baekje. However, their ancestors had originally used wooden chopsticks. There are several theories as to how and why metal chopsticks came to predominate in Korea. One is that a lack of high-quality wood for making wooden chopsticks led to the victory of metal by virtue of its cheapness. Others argue that hygiene was a deciding factor, though there is no obvious evidence that the Korean public's concept of hygiene in premodern times was any higher or lower than in China and Japan, where wooden chopsticks were and are still used. Another theory is that gold, silver, copper, and other metals became symbols of power and wealth after the Iron Age. This led Korean aristocrats and wealthy people to begin using gold or silver utensils. Eventually, metal became more affordable with the mass production of the 20th century.

One final theory is that chopsticks evolved in line with the foods of the countries where people used them. The Chinese and Japanese enjoy noodles and fried food, and metal chopsticks are not as suitable for such dishes because they tend to slide off the utensil. In contrast, Korean foods require precise timing, concentration, and dexterity—especially when they deal with such tearing-resistant fare as kimchi or *muk* (acorn jelly).

There is one additional interesting theory on Koreans' use of metal chopsticks. During an interview at the height of his career, Professor Hwang Woo-suk of Seoul National University, notorious for duping the world with claims that he had produced embryonic stem cells, said, "In the entire world, which nationality other than Koreans can pick up beans with metal chopsticks?" He was referring to the claim that Korean researchers were the first in the world to extract the nucleus of an egg cell, a crucial step in stem cell research. He insisted that this was possible thanks to the skills inherent in Koreans' use of metal chopsticks—researchers, it was argued, were already trained in using their hands for meticulous tasks.

Disgraced scientists aside, the correct handling of metal chopsticks is said to involve the simultaneous use of 30 joints and 50 muscles in the fingers, and it is to the mastery of such complex movements and feats of hand-eye coordination that many of Korea's national successes have been attributed. These include consistently overwhelming victories in the global WorldSkills Competition (such as the recent 2011 round in London), outstanding performance in such high-precision sports as archery and golf, and groundbreaking achievements

in precision-intensive industries like semiconductor production and specialized shipbuilding.

 *Who takes the food trays?*

I live in an apartment complex in Seoul. After lunchtime, I often see empty plates/bowls sitting on a tray on the ground outside the door of my neighbor's apartment (sometimes covered with newspaper). I'm guessing that my neighbor had lunch delivered from a local restaurant. But how does the whole system work, what happens if someone steals the unguarded plates/bowls/tray, and who is responsible for getting them back to the restaurant that they came from? I know these are silly questions, but I'm very curious. Food delivery services in the States use disposable containers.

—Curious in Mapo-gu

 The restaurants' delivery people take the dishes back. Clients are not responsible for any dishes stolen, and the Dude has never heard of a single instance of this happening. It's actually been illegal for the restaurants to use disposable containers

since a whole list of pertinent laws came into effect in 2004. That's why we now see steel chopsticks at Chinese restaurants, where wooden ones were more common in the past. The war on disposable containers has not been limited to restaurants—convenience stores, shops, and public bathhouses have also been affected.

TO TIP OR NOT TO TIP

BY ROBERT KOEHLER

To tip or not to tip. It's one of the most perplexing questions world travelers face as they make their way from country to country. In the United States, seemingly everyone gets tipped. The practice is less common in Europe and Japan. In New Zealand, not only are tips frowned upon, but there are concerns that the influx of foreign tourists—and big-tipping North American ones in particular—might lead to an end to the "no tip" lifestyle enjoyed by locals. Cabbies there have been known to actually "round down" fares, something that would be unheard of in many other countries.

It's difficult to ascertain when the practice of tipping really began, although in Great Britain, it goes back to at least the 15th century. Ironically, the United States was initially hostile to the custom, given its aristocratic overtones. American workers preferred to think of themselves as employees rather than a servant class, and viewed tips as demeaning. It wasn't until the late 1800s that the practice really began in the United States, where it would take root with a vengeance.

When it comes to tipping in Korea, however, the answer is quite simple: you don't. Tipping is not considered customary in Korea. Trying to pass a little extra cash to your waitress or cabbie is likely to be rewarded with a look of bewilderment. In Korea, a value-added tax (VAT) of 10 percent is levied on most goods and services and included in the retail price. Expensive restaurants and hotels may also charge a service fee of 10 percent, although this will be included in the bill, so there's no need to prepare for any other charges than what's written on the bill. Porters at major international restaurants will reportedly accept tips, but they will never "expect" gratuities as is the case in some other nations. Likewise, do not attempt to tip your taxi drivers. Korean taxi drivers prefer to give back exact change, so it's unlikely that you will have your fare "rounded down," and almost never will it be "rounded up." A small tip might be appreciated, however, if your driver goes above and beyond the call of duty. If you've had your cabbie haul your luggage, it might be a good idea to give him a bit extra for his trouble.

A possible exception to the "no tipping" rule is the Itaewon neighborhood. In large part due to its decades spent next to the huge US military base at Yongsan and the large number of foreigners who descend upon the place daily, Itaewon has a culture all its own. Some of its eateries have adopted North American tipping practices, although even here gratuities are strictly optional (i.e., you won't get coffee spilt on your lap for a lousy tip) and probably accepted more with the intention of making foreigners feel more at home than because of a feeling of entitlement on the part of the recipient. That's not to say that service workers in the neighborhood won't welcome your cash, and some places do have tip jars for those feeling particularly generous. Regardless, you will never be expected to provide a tip to anyone in an Itaewon eatery or pub.

2 BOTTOMS UP!

Korea has one of the world's highest consumption rates for alcoholic beverages, rivaling countries like Russia and Romania. In World Health Organization's Global Status Report on Alcohol 2005, Korea ranked among the top 20 countries in the world for consumption in two beverage categories (wine and spirits, including *soju*, or Korean-style vodka). And it's not very surprising, especially considering that Korean venues tend to stay open all hours of the night, and *soju* is literally cheaper than water. It helps that transportation is so convenient in Korea, where travel *sans* one's own vehicle is easy, and even those who bring their car can take advantage of *"daeri unjeon"* services providing drivers for one-time hire.

That, along with the Vegas-style bright and decadent neon lights, is enough to dazzle even the most seasoned drinkers of the US, where alcohol service tends to stop at 2 a.m. Mind you, alcohol is not limited to the conventional post-dark hours. Indeed, it is very prevalent in all areas of society and may even be consumed without much concern at lunchtime business meetings.

Many Westerners will find Korean drinking culture relatively easy to adapt to. And who's to say once expatriates won't return to their home countries, only to dream of their ol' Korea days—albeit with much nebulous haze?

 *What is nightlife like in Korea?*

I'm planning to move to Korea to become an English teacher and am wondering what sort of entertainment is available there. A friend of mine who taught there before assured me that Korea is *the* place for after-hours entertainment. Korean Dude, can you enlighten me on Korean nightlife?

—Ready to Get Crunk

You're right: Korea definitely comes to life once the sun retreats behind the horizon. Nightlife venues offer a wide spectrum of options ranging from traditional to modern, and from loud and upbeat to chill. And whatever you choose to do, you're sure to be good and toasty by the end of the night.

Bars generally come in two varieties: Korean liquor bars and those serving *yangju* (Western liquor). The former categories includes, first and foremost, *soju* (Korean vodka) bars, most of which require customers to order at least one *anju* (appetizer) with their drinks. Other venues include shops selling *makgeolli* (a milky Korean rice wine/beer) and liquors like *baekseju* (Korean medicinal wine) and *maesilju* (refined plum wine). Korea also has several more Western-style bars, including upscale cocktail bars replete with internationally trained mixologists, as well as beer breweries for the average Joe.

Known to enjoy song and dance, young Koreans also frequent a variety of clubs with genres including hip hop, house, rock, and salsa. Clubs in Seoul are found in several districts, with youthful crowds flocking to Hongdae area, upscale partiers to Cheongdam-dong, and international chill-seekers to Itaewon. Remember: clubs are for dancing, while nightclubs are for "booking," or what you could call "enforced flirting."

Since public transportation starts back up around 6 a.m., many partiers prefer to forgo sky-high nighttime taxi charges by finding something to occupy themselves with until they can hop on the subway or bus to get home. Options range from *noraebangs* (Korean karaoke rooms) to the sketchier *DVD bangs* (movie-viewing rooms) and *PC bangs* (Internet cafés). Many, however, opt to relax at a nearby *jjimjilbang* for a good ol' sauna experience and some quick shuteye.

HOTSPOT SEOUL

BY JOEL BROWNING

The Skinny on the Capital's Major Entertainment Districts

There are two major factors that make Seoul one of the liveliest cities in the world after the sun goes down. The first is the diverse nightlife that the intermeshing of the different interests, cultures, and personalities of millions of souls living in close proximity brings. The second is Koreans' need for an outlet after the long hours they put in at work. The latter is the reason that numerous bars, clubs, Internet cafés, and karaoke clubs are open 24 hours a day in every city in Korea. Combined with the former, however, one of the most colorful environments for keeping one's night pumping 'til the crack of dawn is Seoul's nocturnal calling card. The problem (so to speak) for partygoers is not whether they can find a place to go until the sun comes up, but locating that perfect place, tailored for maximum enjoyment to every taste and preference. While there are hot spots aplenty in Seoul, each with its own storied history, atmosphere, and active nightlife, a few in particular deserve mention because of their unique nature.

Itaewon's Globe-Reaching Appeal

Itaewon's most appealing feature is its diversity. The area first earned a reputation for having a predominately American military presence as a result of its proximity to Yongsan Garrison, which houses a good portion of United States Forces Korea. The reality today, however, is that you're just

as likely to meet someone from Pakistan, India, Nigeria, or Russia as you are an American. In no other place in Korea can you find people from such a wide variety of backgrounds. So for those looking for culture in Seoul, Itaewon is as cosmopolitan as you can find. The benefits of this diversity include international cuisine ranging from Egyptian to Mexican, standing gay and straight bars where patrons can mingle and dance while drinking, sports bars showing everything from cricket to hockey, and an environment where transactions can be conducted in almost any language—foremost among them English. (To get there, use any exit at Itaewon Station, Line 6.)

Hongdae's Clubbing Culture

Hongdae is an area named for the school located there, Hongik University, which is famous for its fine arts programs. Apart from the overall creative vibe, the features of Hongdae that tend to draw the largest crowds are the massive number of clubs, the live musical performances, and cheap and plentiful Western alcohol. Clubbing has been a popular activity since the 90s in Hongdae, but it really began to take off in 2001, when a bunch of clubs came up with the idea for "Club Day." At this event, held on the fourth Friday of every month, a 20,000 won pass gains you a ticket for a drink and access to several clubs. Hoping to duplicate this success, live music bars started an event called "Seoul Live Music Festa (SLMF)"— nearly identical to its clubbing counterpart, except it involves live performances and is held on the third or fourth Saturday of every month. Clubbing, dancing, and the cheapest tequila in Korea make Hongdae area one of the hottest spots for Korean college students, English teachers, and foreign students to party. (To get there, take Exit 9 at Hongik Univ. Station, Line 2.)

Gangnam's Privileged Playground

Gangnam, currently home to some of the most affluent members of Korean society, was little more than countryside as recently as 25 years ago. Since that time, however, it's blossomed into a modern and high-end neighborhood where the beautiful leisure class throngs to shop, wine and dine, and see and be seen. The Gangnam area, including the area around Gangnam Station and Apgujeong, is home to some of the poshest wine bars, clubs, cafés, and restaurants in Seoul. It's also where many ethnic Koreans from abroad choose to spend their time. During vacation periods, when children from well-heeled families return home and mix with these overseas Koreans, one is just as likely to hear English spoken as Korean. So whether you want to dance the night away in a fancy club like Eden or try your hand at "booking" in a nightclub like Boss, Gangnam has what you're looking for—if you can afford it. (To get there, go to Sinsa Station, Line 3.)

Daehangno's Theatrical Charms

Daehangno, or "University Road," is the area that used to be adjacent to Seoul National University before it moved its main campus south to Gwanak-gu. The standout feature here is the sheer number of live performance acts that can be found. A walk down the alleys and byways of this youth-oriented area is, like most other Seoul neighborhoods, home to numerous clubs, cafés, and bars, but it also reveals theaters and stages of varying scale for musicals, plays, and other live theatrical performances in equal measure. Walls are plastered with advertisements for these performances, and many of those found partying in Daehangno are audience members who've stuck around long after curtain call. (To get there, head to Hyehwa Station on Line 4.)

 *Is alcohol a drug in Korea?*

I have lived in Korea for seven months and I am curious about Korean attitudes towards alcohol. I have asked several Koreans about alcohol, and most of them think that it is not a drug. This confounds me; as an American, I was inculcated with a Puritan belief that all intoxicants, despite their legality, are drugs. Almost every time I bring up the idea that alcohol is a drug to a Korean, I am immediately and vehemently pinned against the wall for my sacrilegious proclamation: "You're wrong! *Soju* isn't addictive! It isn't a drug because it's legal!" I am wondering what your take on all this is.

—Rollin' in Gangnam

 In a visit to Seoul to a few years back, the Hong Kong actress Karen Mok joked that she should get treated for all the *soju* she drank in Korea. Mok, who had played a drug addict in the musical *RENT*, compared the drink with a drug. As for whether it actually is, the answer is "sort of"—it's addictive, and it influences people's behavior, often in a bad way. Many Koreans, however, tend to see it as a way to relieve the stress

of daily life. The mass media, especially TV miniseries and movies, show scenes of *soju* drinking with alarming frequency. And the public, enthralled by all the romanticism, has grown to underestimate the power and addictiveness of the substance.

Q *What is the attitude toward alcohol in Korea?*

Call me not-so-well-traveled, but I have never been to a country where it is not considered outrageous to open a bottle of vodka (or *soju*) in broad daylight. As much as Koreans love getting smashed, however, there does seem to be some protocol when it comes to drunken pleasures. Tell me, how integral is alcohol to Korean social life, and why?

—Ethanol Ethics

A

Drinking is not so much a highway to inebriation as it is a very communal activity encouraging deeper connections between people. In a country still ruled by Confucianism, citizens often must restrain themselves according to strict etiquette; younger members of society are encouraged to be quiet and reserved, particularly in the presence of elders. While there are still age-based hierarchical guidelines when it comes to drinking, alcohol nevertheless serves as a way to break through constrained exteriors, and participants often feel more comfortable, even around strangers, after drinking it. On a related note, fathers consider it a great honor to pour their grown son his first glass of alcohol, an act that is seen as heralding his coming of age and becoming a fellow man of society. It's a proud moment for any father.

Alcohol is also an integral part of business, where meetings are often conducted with alcohol present, and even educational life, with coworkers and school colleagues frequently engaging in *hoesik*—literally, workplace dining and drinking. A popular food-and-alcohol combination is *samgyeopsal* (Korean-style bacon) with *soju*. By breaking down walls through alcohol and allowing individuals to speak more honestly and candidly with each other, business and school colleagues can often strengthen *jeong* (emotional attachment) even between *seonbae* (older colleagues) and *hubae* (younger colleagues), build team spirit, and promote communal culture. Since the days of yore, Koreans have always enjoyed song and dance with their dining and drinking. This may be why karaoke at a *noraebang* (singing room) is a frequent follow-up to *hoesik* festivities. Of course, alcohol is also a quick way to relieve the stress experienced in a highly competitive and hard-working society.

Finally, alcohol has commonly been referred to in Korea as a "cure-all" for ailments such as nerves and depression. Its alleged medicinal effects—such as improving and increasing blood flow—have traditionally been given much credence.

Q Do I have to share my alcohol glass?

I once went out drinking with some adult students. One man drank some alcohol out of a glass. The glass was refilled, and he then offered it to me. In Western countries, people never drink out of the same glass. We think that it's unsanitary and can lead to the spread of diseases. (In fact, some Koreans have begun to promote the fact that used *soju* glasses can transfer hepatitis.) I was about to explain this to him when he said, "I know that Western people don't like to do this because you think it's unsanitary. However, we are in Korea, and you must do as Koreans do." I don't understand why he was trying to impose his culture on me, especially since my reservations were based on health concerns.

—The Hygienist

According to Professor Nam Tae-woo of Chung-Ang University, there are three ways to drink alcohol with friends: 1) to pour and drink as much alcohol as you want in your own glass whenever you want it (as in Western countries and Japan); 2) to toast a drinking partner with glasses (Russia or China); and 3) to share glasses with partners as a token of respect for the elder and as a gesture indicating the closeness of friends (Korea). Korea may be the only country that follows the tradition of sharing your glass. This unique culture is said to originate from the ancient custom of the *hwarang*, or young noblemen during the Silla Dynasty (BC 57–935), who floated glasses that were two-thirds filled with alcohol on the doughnut-shaped pond in Poseokjeong, Gyeongju. As the ground was on an incline, the *hwarang* took turns picking up glasses while the young noblemen recited poems. Anyone could randomly pick up and drink out of any glass.

Though Koreans believe that this is a way to promote intimacy, many Korean opinion leaders have suggested eradicating this unsanitary drinking habit. In fact, sharing glasses increases the risk of hepatitis infection. Some experts suspect this glass-sharing culture is the main culprit behind the country's high infection rate (70–80%) of *Helicobacter pylori* bacteria. *H. pylori* is cited as a cause of stomach cancer, a disease with a very high rate among the Korean population. In spite of the risks, it seems that Koreans are still not sensitive to the negative health effects of the custom, perhaps due simple to lack of awareness.

I do agree with you: it's up to you not to follow a foreign country's custom when it poses a health risk. In any case, Koreans offer their own glass out of hospitality, so I hope you don't regard it as an offensive gesture.

LEARNING TO LOVE THE "BOMB": KOREA'S *POKTANJU* CULTURE

BY ROBERT KOEHLER

If you've been out drinking with Korean business types, you are no doubt familiar with an evil concoction called the *poktanju*, or "bomb shot." Also known in the West as a "boilermaker" or "depth charge," *poktanju* is born when you drop a shot glass of whiskey into a standard glass of beer. This fearsome firewater is then consumed "bottoms-up" style to get the desired effect, which—to put it bluntly—is to get you drunk fast.

According to the Korean portal site Naver (http://www.naver.com), *poktanju* traces its origins to imperial Russia, where laborers exiled to Siberia drank shots of vodka in beer to chase away the frigid cold. Others find its roots in the United States, where hard-working, hard-drinking miners, dockworkers, and lumberjacks would drink "boilermakers" to get drunk quickly for relatively little money. Either way, this rough drinking culture made its way here via Korean soldiers trained abroad.

It didn't take too long for the "*poktanju* culture" to spread out into Korea's political and economic elite, and eventually into the general business community. As one might expect from a drink that is designed to inebriate in the shortest time possible, the *poktanju* has on occasion led its connoisseurs to engage in textbook examples of poor decision-making. Several years ago, a high-ranking executive at a Korean car company who was attending the media launch of a new model in Australia imbibed more than his fair share of *poktanju* and ended up offering attending journalists half-priced cars. The company was later forced to retract the offer, much to its embarrassment. Another high-ranking official at a human rights watchdog got into hot water after writing a column for a local golf magazine in which he not only bragged of shooting a round of nine after sucking back ten or so boilermakers, but also encouraged readers to do the same. Hunter S. Thompson, rest his soul, would have been proud, but much of Korea's conservative public was not. In fairness to the *poktanju*, the official presumably did write the ill-advised column while he was sober. And, of course, a political and legal mess recently ensued when a local Internet newspaper reported that a lawmaker verbally assaulted a female bar employee following some quality binge drinking. The lawmaker was eventually cleared of the charges (a court found that another figure present at the party made the problematic comments), but not before the heavy-drinking ways of Korea's politicians became a major social issue.

Hankyoreh 21 magazine cited four reasons that Korea's powerful, wealthy, and influential would adopt the *poktanju* as their own. As powerful figures, such individuals wish to feel a sense of unity when they come together, and the *poktanju* is, if nothing else, good at breaking any sense of unease in a quick and efficient manner. Second, the powerful tend to view one another as competitors, and passing around

the *poktanju* glass separates the men from the boys. Third, the wealthy like to show off their privilege by imbibing copious amounts of high-priced imported whiskey or brandy in a carefree manner. Lastly, there is the desire to show off one's masculinity, with the most senior using harsh language to his subordinates or female hosts and forcing them to drink.

Some also point to Korea's *ppalli ppalli* culture as a factor behind the popularity of *poktanju*. Koreans work hard and play even harder; stressed-out office workers want to forget their troubles in the shortest time possible. What they need are "hard drinks for men who want to get drunk fast," and the *poktanju* certainly fits the bill.

If you are unlucky (or lucky, depending on your disposition) to find yourself at a *poktanju* binge, how do you avoid torturing your liver without offending your hosts? In the past, the answer used to be simple: you couldn't. But the times are a-changin', and with them Korea's drinking culture. The Korean media reported some years back that about 30 percent of office workers refused to drink boilermakers, citing the poor economy, the recently implemented five-day workweek (weekday heavy drinking might ruin weekend plans), and health concerns.

What this means is that you are much less likely to find yourself forced to attend a *poktanju* party than in the past, and if you do, you may not be as strongly encouraged to partake in the libations as you would have just a few years ago. If you do get "bombed," however, be prepared for a nasty hangover, the only real treatment for which is rest. On a positive note, Korean bosses tend to be very understanding of hangovers suffered in the line of duty. After a night of work-related hard boozing, just call into the office to tell them you'll be late.

Q *Why is* makgeolli *becoming so popular among drinkers?*

—Ricer

 *Makgeolli*, a traditional rice-based wine among commoners and the nation's oldest liquor, was, until recently, largely neglected and dismissed as a cheap liquor. But now it is returning to glory, with products being marketed as higher-end selections at luxury venues like major department stores and hotels.

There are several reasons for *makgeolli's* newfound popularity. For one, the liquor—which is made from glutinous rice, barley, flour, and wheat steamed with yeast and water and fermented naturally—is being touted as a health drink, with over ten types of amino acids, vitamin B, inositol, cholin, and a high protein content. It has also been shown to contain an organic compound that is effective in quenching thirst, invigorating the metabolism, relieving fatigue, and improving one's complexion. This would explain why *makgeolli* was traditionally so popular among farmers, who would often drink it in place of food to sustain them throughout their day of hard labor.

More than anything, though, it's the creamy texture and soft and sweet taste that draw people to this rice wine. A good *makgeolli* is supposed to blend well with most other side dishes, leaving only a cool aftertaste. Since makgeolli is low in

alcohol content (only six to seven percent), the drink is good for those who are not as strongly weathered to strong alcohol.

Makgeolli certainly has sped ahead in sales records, showing a 2011 growth rate in sales of 30%. The amount exported to neighboring Japan has surpassed the amount of sake exported to Korea in 2010. This may be partly thanks to Bae Yong-joon, a Korean actor who is wildly popular in Japan. When Bae opened two restaurants in Japan, he sold out their limited set of *makgeolli* (300 packs of six bottles) in a mere eight minutes.

SURVIVING THE MORNING AFTER

BY ANDREW PETTY

Pharmacies are abundant in Seoul. There are even some inside a few subway stations, answering the prayer of many people suffering from Korea's most common work-related injury—the hangover. A few rounds of *poktanju* after hours on the company's tab, even on weekday nights, is not too unusual.

I can't speak a lick of Korean, but I can walk into a drug store, grab my head in a vise grip, and tell the pharmacist "*sukchwi.*" With a laugh, he will instantly understand me. He returns with a neon-labeled brown bottle and a pouch full of what seems like rabbit food. *Sukchwi* means something like "pickled in alcohol," and should be listed on page two of the traveler's Korean phrase book, given the nation's love affair with drinking. Rarely in other countries are people so readily forgiven for showing up to work an hour late after having drinks with the boss. Here, you do not find the kind of social stigma on binge drinking that you would in, say, Syria. It's not just a stereotype. A Seoul National University professor found that Korea has the highest percentage of adult alcoholics in the world, defining one in every five Korean men as an alcoholic. Let's hope they never survey expats, who could certainly rival that statistic.

According to research by a former *Korea Herald* reporter, the quest for the perfect hangover cure has continued through the ages, from ancient Romans eating owl eggs to modern day Puerto Ricans rubbing

lemon juice on their armpits. Korea deserves some honorary recognition for its attempts, too. The rabbit food my pharmacist gave me is actually condensed herbs containing alder and mountain ash, grown in Korea. The herbs promote the oxidation of acetaldehydes and/or ethyl alcohols so that they don't remain in the liver. Basically, it detoxifies your system. Not bad, eh? When you take it with the medicine bottle, you are likely to pass a few more poisonous toxins, and then you are on your way to recovery.

Or maybe it's all in your mind? Like the miracle cures sold in the 19th century that turned out to be liquor and soda, these wonder drinks are sold with the same marketing smoke and mirrors. With names like "Drinker's Magician" and "Millennium Business Partner," they're after the desperate customer who will pay up to 5,000 won for an ounce of relief. Some of them claim to have FDA licenses or "certificates," and pharmacists will not discourage you from buying them. One said that whatever the science, if the potions make people believe they feel better, then why not sell them? But why turn to modern science, anyway, when you have 5,000 years of wisdom at your fingertips in Korea? One classic miracle drug here is ginseng. (Surprise, surprise! It even cures hangovers.) Korea Gingseng MFG. Co., Ltd. claims their crop normalizes changes in the liver cells, breaks down lactic acid, and aids in hydration when taken after drinking. Sounds nutritious, but is it strong enough to reduce the jackhammering pain felt after a night of "one shots?"

Sometimes I prefer the pure honesty of a local *ajumma*, who usually recommends a spicy bowl of *haejangguk*, which includes beef and bones, ground hot pepper, and bean sprouts. The active agent here is actually the bean sprouts, containing aspartic acid that can remove poisons from the blood stream. But my favorite hangover cure belongs in the "nonscientific" category. Koreans have their own version of the ol' hair of the dog: *haejangsul*. A co-worker recommended drinking an extra shot of *soju* after getting out of bed, this time with a hint of pepper. Then I add my own special touch: settling the stomach with a greasy lunch of McDonald's French fries.

Of course, binge drinking—or liquor, period—is not for everybody. Don't worry: in a country where Asian glow is not so much Asian glow as ubiquitous glow, there are many more healthful options for drinking, too.

Q *What kind of tea is it?*

I'm looking for the name of a specific tea. It's black and thick, and its bitter taste is close to licorice. Apparently, it's a kind of herb tea, served with candied ginger. Do you have any idea what it could be?

—Teapsy

A

It's not a tea, but a medicine, though there are some shops that sell it like a tea. It's called *sipjeon daebotang*, a Korean herbal medicine made out of ten different herbs, including ginseng and licorice. Originally, it's supposed to revitalize your energy and circulation. It's especially good for those who have sensitive stomachs and suffer from cold feet and hands. Such people, who include many Koreans, are categorized as *soeumin* according to Korea's traditional Sasang Constitutional Medicine. Generally, Westerners have a different body constitution.

The easiest way to find out if any type of medicine is good for your health is to check how your body reacts to it. Since it's medicine, you may experience side effects, such as fever, headache, and drowsiness, especially if you indulge without a proper prescription from an herbal doctor.

Q *Why is coffee so expensive in Korea?*

—Caffeine High

Drinking coffee became popular in the 1950s, right after the Korean War, due to the influence of American culture, although Emperor Gojong, the 26th king of the Joseon Dynasty, used to enjoy a good cup of java as he kicked back in Deoksugung Palace's Western-style Jeonggwanheon Pavilion. Purely imported coffee started as an expensive drink. Because there

was an existing tea culture prior to the introduction of coffee, and Koreans tend to gather together to converse, the custom of drinking coffee was picked up rather easily, resulting in a slew of coffee shops all around the country. These coffee houses have only recently been replaced by Starbuckses and Coffee Beans. For foreign coffee chains, the high coffee price is due to royalties and high cost of rent in Seoul.

 *Any decaffeinated coffee?*

I was wondering why decaffeinated coffee is not available in Seoul. Sometimes you can find decaf instant coffee at the supermarket, but the local coffee shops, and even some franchise coffee shops, do not carry decaf. I know many locals who would drink it, as I would, in the evening when it is too late for caffeine.

 The Dude found that decaffeinated coffee is simply not that popular here. In fact, some people don't even know what decaf coffee is. This is why most coffee shops don't carry decaf. If you need decaf late at night, there are some coffee chains (but only select branches such as Starbucks and Coffee Bean) that do

carry it. But the search is likely to be so bothersome that you are better off purchasing the instant variety from a supermarket or convenient store.

MAKE YOURSELF AT HOME

1 HOME SWEET HOME

A h, home. Just hearing the word evokes visions of a verdant garden in the backyard, the sounds of a lovely fireplace crackling away in the corner, and the aroma of a delicious casserole cooking away in the oven, doesn't it? WRONG. You're in Korea now, and you're playing a whole different game. No more bowls of Doritos and wearing shoes in the house; here come the *yo*s and massive deposits! Beginning with some tips on renting (since you need a place to live, right?), the Dude will do his best to help you rediscover that sense of home sweet home—albeit with that fire-hot *ondol* floor.

SLEEPLESS IN SEOUL

BY NANCY KIM

Rip Van Winkle managed to sleep on the damp forest floor of the Catskills for thirty years. If you are like me, though, you probably need a sleeping surface and bedding that are a little more ergonomically friendly. (Remember, Rip had the help of large quantities of a mysterious Dutch liquor brewed by Catskill natives to withstand decades of bedless sleep.)

Thousands of miles away from upstate New York, Koreans have traditionally slept on a futon called a *yo* and a cotton-stuffed comforter called an *ibul*. Many Koreans still do, storing them in a closet. Western-style beds are commonplace these days, as is Western-style bedding like comforters, duvet covers, and fitted sheets.

Flat sheets, on the other hand, are extremely rare. During my hunt for a flat sheet, I managed to locate a couple on the upper floors of high-end department stores, where household items are sold. Unfortunately, they were mind-blowingly expensive, running over 100,000 won apiece, and the selection was extremely limited. At Namdaemun Market, I only managed to find one flat sheet, which was as thick as a mattress pad and came only in king-size.

All in all, if you are a little more particular about your sleeping environment than Rip Van Winkle and will go so far as to say you need a sheet between you and your comforter, your best bet is to either have someone ship it or bring it to you from a flat sheet-friendly location.

Q *Why should I take off my shoes when entering a Korean home?*

Koreans take off their shoes before entering temples, certain restaurants and private apartments and houses. There are very practical reasons for this—hygiene, for one. You can imagine the dirt and grime that can come from trekking outdoors all day in shoes. Also, who wants to be wearing their shoes around all day? (Haven't you heard that it's better for humans to walk barefoot?)

Koreans, however, are especially sensitive to dirty floors because of their traditional *ondol* under-floor heating system. Many Westerners still seem to be unaware of this form of heating, although many more environmentally constructed homes in the US are utilizing similar technology these days.

Thanks to the coziness of heated floors, it is still common Korean practice to sit on the floor. If anything, sitting—and walking barefoot on such floors, for that matter—allows you to feel the full warmth of the *ondol* floor through your feet. So ingrained is this custom of removing shoes that even in the more Western-style homes, it is considered very disrespectful to enter with your shoes on.

It is interesting to note that the sitting culture resulting from *ondol* floors influenced the design of Korean traditional dress—*hanbok* was made loose so as to leave enough room for people to easily bend their knees and sit for long periods of time, and traditional shoes were made in such a way that they were easy to take off and put on.

THE BARE (FOOT) NECESSITIES

BY SCOTT FALLIS

It had been two years since I visited my parents in New York City. As soon as I entered the apartment, I immediately and instinctively pulled the laces on my shoes toward myself, grabbed the heel, and pulled off the footwear, setting it down on a narrow stretch of carpeting to the left side of the door. My wife and son followed suit. My mother met us in the living room and stared down at our shoeless feet in stunned amazement. In her mind, we had committed a faux pas.

I explained to my mother that people in Korea always remove their footwear upon entering a house, out of respect and to keep the place clean. She found this somewhat incomprehensible.

I could understand her point of view, since I had worn shoes inside my apartment since early childhood. I had only learned about the Asian custom of removing shoes after traveling across the Pacific in search of adventure and employment. Removing shoes had become so natural to me that I couldn't bear to put them on again and contribute further to the dust and dirt ingrained in a once-beautiful carpet.

I pointed out all the stuff that collects on the bottom of footwear— chewing gum, dirt, mud, and whatever else someone spilled, dropped, or left on the sidewalk, not least among them doggie droppings. A pair of Nike Air Jordans, for example, has crevices, grooves, and holes enough to serve as a household vacuum cleaner, collecting unwanted junk like the tiny pebbles I used to pick out from the plastic bottom of my sneakers with a small steak knife. I told my mother about the cloth slippers worn in most rooms, and the hard plastic ones slipped on for the bathroom. My mother considered all this an unnecessary hassle and waste of time.

My wife had a brilliant idea. We went to a nearby convenience store and picked up slippers to wear throughout our stay. I must admit, though, that it bothered me whenever guests came to visit and wore shoes inside the apartment. While I couldn't get used to them, they mostly thought it strange that we were wearing slippers.

In the future, I plan a permanent return to the United States. How will I handle the shoe issue in my own house? Obviously, we will have both Korean and American friends. Koreans will understand the principle of removing their shoes. Our American friends may feel somewhat uncomfortable visiting us. We want to respect both Americans and Koreans, and we want them to feel equally welcome in our house. So we will have slippers by the door and ask everyone to remove their shoes and use them. If some Americans really have trouble with this, like my mother (who couldn't walk well on carpeting while wearing loose-fitting slippers), we will allow them to wear their shoes and do a proper cleaning once they leave.

The Korean custom of removing footwear upon entering a house is far more hygienic. By removing shoes, we keep many kinds of harmful germs out of the home. I can only hope this wonderful cultural trait becomes trendy back in the United States and is eventually adopted as proper living etiquette. America and Korea have influenced each other's culture for generations. Unfortunately, this influence has been far too one-sided. A river flows in only one direction, but the ocean flows in several. Like the oceans that divide us, culture and customs need to be identified, evaluated, and considered for implementation. The custom of removing one's shoes before entering the home is a perfect example of one Korean custom that should be embraced in my homeland and throughout the world.

Q *Why no dryers?*

I've lived here a few years now, and one thing I truly miss from home is my dryer. I've always wondered why there is a lack of them in Korean homes. Recently, an adult student of mine explained that Koreans think that dryers don't kill the germs the same way the sun does. I asked a reliable Korean friend if there was any validity to this, and was told no—that it was more like "if everyone is buying a white car, so should you." What are your thoughts on this?

—Drying Off

As a lover of fabric softener sheets and hot, toasty clothing, the Korean Dude feels your pain. The first answer as to why dryers are not more widely used that comes to the Dude's mind is that not having one is, ultimately, far more economical. Another thing is limited space, since most Koreans today live in small flats.

Basically, Koreans don't seem to feel a need for this household appliance. Many also argue that dryers break down fabric quicker. They claim that towels become less absorbent and clothing shrinks if put them through the drying cycle. The Dude knows of a Seoul housewife who lived in the US for some time and claims she only needs the dryer for ten days during the rainy summer season.

Funny that drying clothing is the one thing Koreans aren't all *ppalli ppalli* about.

 *What are the usual gifts for housewarming parties?*

I was recently invited to the housewarming party of my labmate, and I'm stumped about what I should get as a gift. Any suggestions, Korean Dude?

—The Giver

A There are several options for housewarming gifts, which generally err on the practical side. Two popular practical gifts also have symbolic meanings. Laundry detergent froths up into lots of bubbles, representing prosperity. Toilet paper is long and unrolls continuously and smoothly; this is meant to symbolize life unfolding smoothly for the new occupant of the home.

For healthy eaters, fruit is appreciated. Potted plants may be a good choice for green-lovers. For example, *Sansevieria trifasciata*, also known as the snake plant, is known for requiring minimal upkeep and being able to remove toxins like nitrogen oxide and formaldehyde.

Other popular gifts include earthenware sets, coffee makers, wine, wall clocks, tool sets, fire extinguishers, and cake. Some gift choices may depend on the situation of the recipients. The elderly will enjoy comfort accessories such as long underwear and heated massagers. Newlyweds may appreciate scented candles or a set of coffee cups and saucers.

If you're going to the party as a group, you might consider pooling money to buy slightly pricier items, such as a microwave oven or an electronic bidet.

Note that housewarming gifts are also given by new residents of homes and even businesses. In fact, new residents bring red bean rice cakes to their new neighbors as a way of establishing good relations and laying the foundation for harmonious collective living.

LOOKING YOUR OWN GIFT HORSE IN THE MOUTH

BY JOANNE YUN

I've always been a little bemused by the paradoxes that can accompany the ritual of gift-giving. Consider the American holiday season and the schizophrenic barrage of clichés that pervades it. "Find the perfect gift" to "show how much you care"! Oh, but don't forget that it's not really the gift—"it's the thought that counts." No wonder people go crazy during the holidays. The "it's the thought that counts" philosophy seems like a copout; if you're really being thoughtful, shouldn't you be able to somehow find the perfect gift? So my tendency is to obsess over finding that unique, special present that will delight its recipient and, of course, validate me as the most thoughtful person ever!

During my time in Korea, however, I've had to change my attitude, as I realize that gift-giving involves cultural ideas about values and relationships that can confound a foreigner who has no clue about either. The giving of gifts is a common ritual in Korean culture, taking place on occasions from birthdays to "White Days" to "meeting the parents of your future spouse" days. For foreigners new to Korea, giving gifts when you meet Korean people can make a great first impression.

We ETAs (Fulbright English Teaching Assistants) eagerly noted that laundry detergent and fruit juice made good gifts for the Korean families that we might visit. We stuffed suitcases with gifts to give to our as-yet-unknown host families and school staff. We were ready to shower our communities with love to create some *jeong*—the Korean word for that unspoken emotional bond between people.

Just before Chuseok last year, word spread that giving our school principal a gift for the holiday would be a nice, culturally savvy gesture. When I asked my co-teacher what he thought, he replied, "Yes, that's a good idea," and estimated that I would need to spend 30,000 won. His suggestion as to what I should get: "What about socks?"

I was baffled. Was I supposed to buy 30 pairs of socks? Five pairs of really nice socks? And what was my principal's taste in socks? Granted, older Korean men don't seem to vary too much in terms of personal style, so I could probably have guessed. But I couldn't see myself buying a man in his sixties socks—something that I mentally grouped with underwear.

I pressed him: "Any other suggestions?" My co-teacher thought for another moment and then came up with "liquor," which I felt slightly more optimistic about. At least he would enjoy it, I reasoned. I headed to the grocery store. Unfortunately, they didn't seem to have any nice liquor available. However, something else caught my eye: an impressive ginseng honey gift set that a salesperson assured me would be both healthy and appropriate. Perfect! Armed with that and two monstrous boxes of grapes for the teachers' room, I struggled into school the next day, excited to see how my gifts would be received. The honey was accepted with a polite "You shouldn't have! But thank you," and the grapes were gone by second period.

I felt a little deflated and, for a while, worried that perhaps I hadn't done things quite right. Instead, I realized that in Korea, the giving and receiving of gifts simply aren't accompanied by the same meanings as in the United States. It may be because gifts are given more frequently in

Korea, and to people that are less well known; it may be because there is less of a culture of openly expressing gratitude for gifts. After all, *jeong* is hard to pin down because it is so often unspoken.

For an American like me, I think "unspoken" usually translates to something imperceptible. Either way, I no longer expect that my noble quest to find the "perfect gift" will be rewarded with expressions of gratitude, or a tangible sense that I've earned some *jeong* points. To save myself further stress, I'm not going to obsess over gifts anymore. I've sought refuge in thinking that it's the thought that counts. So the next time a holiday rolls around, I will go to the department store and thoughtfully pick up a nice gift set of socks.

Q *Why do old people take care of recycling?*

Rather than trucks, most of the recycling in my neighborhood is handled by old people with pushcarts, or even old baby strollers. What are the economics behind that system?

—On Garbage Duty

There are recycling companies who should be doing the job. Of course, they make some money out of gathering glass bottles, papers, and aluminum cans, but apparently their profits don't cover the cost. So old people are taking up the job. Some of the old people I know are doing it partly because they think it's wasteful not to recycle such things. We should remember that Korea has reached the current status quo thanks to their generation's mindset, which allowed the nation to survive hard times. The Dude also thinks it's a shame that so many disposable cups and utensils go unrecycled at US hamburger restaurants.

 *How do you borrow books in English?*

I love reading books very much, but I'm spending a fortune getting all the books I want to read from Kyobo Bookstore. Doesn't Korea have an English language library? Where can I go to borrow books (contemporary and classic) for free?

—BookWorm

In Seoul, there are 22 municipal public libraries where you can take books home, but just a handful of English titles are available. One good thing, though, is that you can propose particular book titles to purchase. *Gus* (wards) also have public libraries, where the situation is very similar.

Seoul Selection Bookshop near Gyeongbokgung Palace has a small used book corner where you can find some English titles on Korea at very reasonable prices. There are also a couple of second-hand bookshops in Itaewon where you can acquire English books at modest prices.

As far as an extensive English and foreign language book collections are concerned, the National Library of Korea, located in Seocho-dong, could be a good resource. It has 1,065,406 foreign publications (as of 2012), or 12.5 percent of its total catalogue. English information is provided on its website at http://www.nl.go.kr. One caveat: it is a reference library, meaning books cannot be signed out and taken home. They can only be read on the premises. But it has an e-book service, too, so you can easily borrow e-books if you've got the devises for it.

2 DIGITAL GET DOWN

G iven that it's possibly the most digitally wired country in the world, it is near impossible to get by in Korea without a cell phone. Since so many services and functions are linked digitally, it is basically imperative for everyone in Korea to have access to digital services.

And while cable TV might not be quite as essential, it will likely be your main source of knowledge on popular culture, providing fodder for perhaps 80 percent of your conversations with local Koreans.

Q *Are answering machines a rarity in Korea, or what?*

When I lived in Korea, I had a land line with an answering machine that would pick up when I wasn't there to answer.

Very frequently, I would arrive home and hit the play button, only to receive a message or two with a Korean saying, "*Yeoboseyo? Yeoboseyo? Yeoboseyo?*" sometimes for up to 20 or 30 seconds. It was almost as if the caller did not quite get the fact that the voice they had heard was a recording and that they were supposed to leave a message or hang up.

—Deleting Obsolete Voice Mails

Yes, some Korean homes, and many offices, use answering machines. Nowadays, many people have abandoned landlines and gone completely mobile, which has made voice mail service even easier to use. If you recorded your message in English, there is a possibility that your caller didn't understand what you had recorded. If you recorded it in Korean, then I'm stumped.

Why should I pay a year in advance for a cable hookup?

This problem is not limited to cable, or to me. I think every foreigner has had to put up with being asked to pay more

before anything is sold or service given. Is this legal? Is there any way to fight the system? Why should I pay $200 for my cable hookup when my Korean neighbors pay much less for the same service? "Because you're a foreigner" is a rather sorry excuse for price gouging.

—Face/Off with the Cable Guy

 The Korean Dude doubted your question until he called cable companies and chatted with some sweet-talking customer consultants from several cable TV, Internet, and telephone companies. They said that payment systems differ among individual companies. The Dude only found one satellite TV broadcaster that seemed to discriminate against foreigners. Also, some cable companies demanded that new foreign subscribers prepay up to six or twelve months in advance. The Dude tried contacting the Korean Broadcasting Commission, which is in charge of TV-related regulations. It said the prepayment requirement for foreigners is not an official regulation adopted by its civil affairs department. The staff even sounded surprised at hearing of the discrimination against foreigners and suggested that the Dude present a written petition to them. The Dude guesses that companies may believe foreigners are likely to just take off without paying their bill, and are therefore a potential risk. But if you file a complaint by calling Korea Communications Commision (02-1335), you can fight this unfair practice.

3 THE OFFICE

Office politics. Gotta love'em.

NOT. But they are an inevitable part of working life that no worker can escape. Depending on your perspective, corporate culture may or may not be more difficult to deal with in Korea. Consider several facts:

• Koreans are known for being very hard-working, meaning that you need to think and act fast, and endure a lot of (often uncompensated) overtime.

• Koreans practice total subservience to superiors. While some may find the custom of destroying creativity at the hands of "what the upper echelons want" stifling, others may find it easier to bow to greater powers.

• Koreans indulge in a good deal of inter-company relations— tiresome for the private, but wonderful for those who, say, have no friends outside the office. Also a good excuse to drink on the company's dime.

This list could go on and on and on. But the Korean Dude feels that testimony may serve to hammer home the truth of Korean corporate culture more effectively.

The following includes two essays presented by two well-informed, insightful women who have insider knowledge of Korean working culture. May their words be a warning—or an encouragement—to you, job seeker!

BUSINESS CULTURE IN KOREA:
A LITTLE KNOWLEDGE GOES A LONG WAY IN CREATING A GOOD OFFICE ATMOSPHERE

BY KELLI DONIGAN

When it comes to working in Korea, whether it's at a school, trade company, or one of the big Korean conglomerates, business and making money are taken seriously. The Korean workplace can be competitive and fierce, with grueling hours and many non-verbal nuances and unforeseen expectations. At the same time, the working environment can be harmonious and collective. Korean companies pride themselves on the fact that there is a foreigner working in their company, but often lack a foreigner's know-how and perspective on improving international business relations. Here are some helpful insights on how Korean business culture works.

Hierarchical and Collective Structure

Korean society still preserves many Confucian beliefs in daily life and in business. Hierarchical and collective structures lay the foundation for relationships and ways of conducting business. Know who's above you and who's below you, and interact respectfully with your superiors.

Age and seniority are also quite important to someone's status in a company, where positions were traditionally assigned based on those two elements, as well as male gender. Note that the situation has improved: businesses are adapting to Western standards, adopting the five-day work week and promoting qualified women and younger employees more to higher positions.

Not Exactly 9 to 6: Expect Some Overtime

Although your contract conditions may specify hours from 9 a.m. to 6 p.m., this is not always the case in practice. Koreans are somewhat more lenient with foreigners, who are not expected to "be Korean" per se, so if you leave at the time you agreed upon, it should be fine. However, when there's a lot of work to be done or everyone else is staying behind, it's also good to volunteer some overtime, even if not asked formally.

Leaving an assignment unfinished before heading home is very much frowned upon. Koreans expect assignments to be finished completely before the end of the day. In this situation, it's best to explain that you must leave at a certain time for something important prior to or upon receiving your assignment, but it's advisable to stay a little longer and offer some compromise or alternative arrangement.

Company Dinners, Outings, and MT: Truly Mandatory?

Korean businesses are not all work and no play. Companies always find time to schedule company dinners (called *hoesik*), workshops, or MT (Membership Training) for mutual bonding. Koreans consider such outings important in building good relations with colleagues and superiors, as well as sharing laughs, drinks, and ideas about the company.

Although such events are not mandatory—just strongly encouraged— you may be pressured to go by close colleagues, since it's a collective activity, and they may also find it unfair that you are let off the hook. Some companies actually coordinate these events exclusively for Korean

employees. In any case, it's important to learn some Korean to help you interact with your Korean colleagues on a professional and personal level.

Relationships in the Workplace

This brings us to relationships in the workplace. Relationships, which are often developed through a considerable amount of drinking and eating, are vital in doing business in Korea. Because most of your time is spent at work, it's good to contribute to your company's efforts to promote a family-like atmosphere. However, it's wise to stay out of office politics and gossip if you can. If you start dating one of your coworkers, keep things low-key. Also, suck up—but not too much—to your superiors or boss. Just be yourself, and show that you're serious about your job. This will help Koreans recognize and respect you as an individual who stands out, and not just because you're the foreigner.

Is it common to have paychecks mailed directly to an employee's parents?

Is it true that business owners will mail the paycheck of a young, unmarried woman directly to her parents? (I was told this by our private academy's supervisor.) Korean/foreign relationships are sometimes tense, and I wonder if she made this up to gain the Korean teachers' empathy.

The Korean Dude has never heard of this. Though young Korean women are regarded as dependent on their parents before marriage, he has heard of no company requiring a female employee to agree to send her paycheck directly to her parents. If she wished to do so, on the other hand, the company can wire the pay to her parents' account. In a few cases, the Dude has observed young men and women willingly allow their parents to take control of their income and receive allowances. But again, this is not mandatory, and it's fairly rare. You should talk about this with your academy's supervisor if they pushed you to do the same.

A WOMAN'S RESPONSE TO CORPORATE KOREA

BY JUNE KIM

When I heard about my friend's entry-level training program at a prestigious Korean conglomerate, the first thing that came to mind was "cult." For two months, entry-levels are whisked away to a training facility outside of Seoul. *What was this, the army?*

Let me give you a quick rundown. Participants are subjected to grueling daily schedules that begin at 5:30 a.m. and may not end until the wee morning hours of the next day. New initiates are educated on the company's history and culture and participate in various group activities. Etiquette classes aimed at producing well-rounded international businessmen teach wine tasting and proper greetings. At the office, employees are instilled with corporate spirit through constant playback of the company anthem and company news.

A foreign employee of a Korean company tried to put a positive spin on this: "Western companies don't encourage team building with the same intensity as Korean organizations." Indeed, employees become like family, with friendships flourishing easily among colleagues.

As of 2004, Korean workers were only legally obligated to work 40 hours per week. But have shortened work hours changed Korean corporate culture's silent pressure on employees to give unpaid extra work and time? Taking advantage of your annual leave allowance still has to be done with great tact. Taking too many days off is frowned upon, and priority for the best vacation days is still given to superiors.

This company-first mentality permeates social gatherings. Company dinners (*hoesik*) occur much too frequently for many family members of corporate workers. While they can make great teambuilding opportunities, many workers are de facto without choice about attending and cannot leave before their superiors. Some even shoulder the responsibility of seeing their superiors home after a long night of alcohol and karaoke.

Some point to the company-first mentality and strict corporate hierarchy in Confucian tradition, and even military conscription. The Korean language, whether as a reflection of hierarchical culture or its catalyst, is an omnipresent reminder of an individual's status on the corporate ladder. Colleagues refer to each other by title and surname rather than by given name. A superior may call a subordinate "Lee *gwajang*" ("Section Chief Lee"), while Lee's subordinates would call him "*gwajangnim*" (-*nim* is a suffix that expresses higher status). Company hierarchy determines everything—even where people sit within the office and what hotels they can stay at while on business trips.

Another unique characteristic of Korean corporate culture is bonuses, regular handouts that form a significant portion of one's annual income. A worker making two million won a month can expect a bonus of some 1.5 million won around major holidays such as New Year's and Chuseok (Korean Thanksgiving). Many companies also have profit-sharing bonuses. The amount depends on the performance of your department or section (emphasizing teamwork over individual performance) and can be as much as 50 percent of your annual salary.

As alien as training camps and all-night company drinking may seem to outsiders, corporate culture is, in the end, merely a set of stylized human behavior. Isn't human life in general fascinatingly alien when you give it some closer examination?

4 STAYING ALIVE

Q What is the Korean medical insurance system like?

I've heard it said that Korea has an excellent medical care system, even without the excess of equipment and wonderfully expensive insurance policies of countries like the US. What's so special about medical insurance in Korea?

—A New Patient

A   Explaining the entire medical insurance system to you would require long, technical perambulations about each and every service and benefit. To sum it up in a few short words, however, Korea has a very advanced universal health care system that is run by the National Health Insurance Corporation (NHIC), which administers national health insurance—managing enrollment, setting medical fee schedules through negotiations with providers, and providing health insurance benefits.

The program covers the entire population as part of a compulsory social insurance system. Enrollment is mandatory for all Koreans residing in Korean territory, except for some Medical Aid beneficiaries. This helps to reduce the cost of insurance for each individual, as well as the cost of medical services overall. In addition, many clinics will, on an individual basis, offer free clinic visits if there is nothing wrong with the patient. Nifty, isn't it?

Also notable is the fact that patients can select their practitioner or medical care institution. When a patient wants to receive medical care from a secondary hospital (specialized general hospital), they must present a referral slip issued by the doctor who saw them first. Exceptions in the referral system are granted in the case of childbirth, emergency medical care, dental care services, rehabilitation, family medicine services, and medical services for hemophiliacs, in which case any health care institution can be utilized without any limitation.

The Korean Dude would like to add that many doctors here work very quickly and generally offer quality services to patients, although they do have a proclivity for administering the needle. Trypanophobics (i.e., needle-phobes), beware.

Q   *Having a baby in Korea . . .*

I am thinking of getting pregnant, but since I've just arrived in Seoul and don't speak any Korean at all, I still have many doubts. How can I find medical assistance in English? Should I subscribe to some kind of insurance if I decide to have my baby here?

—Aspiring Mother

 You can have your baby here even if you don't have insurance. There are several English-speaking hospitals and clinics. But being without insurance is costly. An employee of Asan Medical Center's international clinic said it's two to three times more expensive than when you have insurance—although birth services are still cheaper than the US in the end. If you or your husband works at a company, you can get insurance through the company. If not, you can register in a regional insurance system by contacting the National Health Insurance Corporation (http://www.nhic.or.kr; homepage has services available in English). In order to find the hospital or clinic nearest to you, you can use the 24-hour Emergency Medical Information Center by calling 1339.

 *What's with all the tests?*

I am six months pregnant and have been receiving excellent medical care at a major hospital here in Seoul. What puzzles me is why the doctors keep checking and testing obsessively for abnormalities. I am young, healthy, in the midst of a normal pregnancy, and neither my husband nor I have any

family history of genetic problems. Nonetheless, doctors were very surprised when I rejected amniocentesis, a level-two ultrasound, and the quad test (used to screen for genetic irregularities). In the US, these are offered to only "high risk" patients. I can't help but wonder what the abortion rate is for "abnormal" pregnancies in Korea, or what the general attitude is toward children with "special needs." I sense that Korean physicians embrace technology and want to offer me everything that is available. But I suspect there may be a routine "weeding out" process. If this is the case, it's quite odd, since there is such a strong Christian element in Korean society today.

—Apprehensive of Doctors

 Doctors are quick to warn against any potential complications that could arise during a pregnancy, mostly because they don't want to take responsibility in emergency cases. It's also true that Koreans these days tend to overestimate the power of science. But the Korean Dude doesn't believe it has anything to do with a "weeding out" process or morality. Yes, it is true that Koreans of the past were obsessed with having male children and disposing of the female children, but this tendency has mostly disappeared from this country with improving gender attitudes. It may be an issue of money, although it doesn't sound like your hospital falls into that category either.

GIVING BACK TO SOCIETY:
WAYS TO VOLUNTEER IN KOREA

BY KELLI DONIGAN

Although volunteering hasn't caught on as feverishly in Korea as, say, learning English, there's a subtle phenomenon happening: small communities are voluntarily taking the time to help each other out.

Spread the Holiday Cheer

In October 2002, a unique store devoted to recycling used goods opened in Seoul's Anguk-dong neighborhood. Due to its popularity, the organization, called the Beautiful Store, has gone on to open and manage several shops nationwide. The Beautiful Store (Areumdaun Gage) is a non-profit NGO that helps people in need with the profits earned from collecting, repairing, and selling second-hand items donated by local residents at a low price. The stores are not just places where goods can be bought and sold; they act as centers for local communities of all different kinds to practice the idea of sharing through profit distribution, as well as the recycling of goods.

Anyone who's interested can become what's called a "donation angel" or an "activity angel" for the Beautiful Store. Donation angels are people who donate articles to the store, and activity angels are those who volunteer to work at one of the shops. Activity angels sell merchandise and maintain the shop, working in morning or afternoon shifts, Monday through Saturday. There are three different ways to become a donation angel: take your goods directly to the store, visit the website to apply (http://www.beautifulstore.org), or call directly at 1577-1113 to have another volunteer from the Beautiful Store come and pick up your donated items.

Little Hands:
Helping the Homeless and Elderly in Korea

Established in May 2004, Little Hands (Jageun Songil) is a non-profit organization dedicated to addressing social problems that don't receive enough public attention and afflict particularly vulnerable members of society. Recently, Little Hands has extended its services to migrant workers who work in Korea, defectors from North Korea, and Korean adoptees who've returned to Korea. How can you lend a hand at Little Hands? Volunteers and members congregate every Wednesday and Saturday at exactly 8 p.m., rain or shine, at Seoul's Euljiro 1-ga subway station. They can be seen handing out rice cakes and coffee to approximately 120 homeless people who sleep at this subway station in cardboard boxes. And every Tuesday and Friday at 2 p.m., you can see Little Hands volunteers giving out snacks and coffee to approximately 400 elderly people at the Jongno 3-ga subway stations. "Volunteers can help by participating and attending these services held by us or through donations," says Kim Kwang-ha, a Little Hands representative. You can also help North Korean defectors learn English. For more information, visit http://cafe.daum.net/samyungdang or call (02) 2235-1717.

Other Meaningful Volunteer Work

Another of the numerous volunteering possibilities is helping out or visiting the House of Sharing (Nanumui Jip). This is a residence for former "comfort women" (women drafted as sexual slaves for the Japanese military during

World War II) located in Gyeonggi-do. Tours are conducted monthly in Korean, Japanese, and English; volunteers who speak any of these languages are always needed, as are translators or editors. Guests are always welcome with reservations. For more information, visit their website at http://www.nanum.org or call (031) 768-0064.

For nature lovers, and mountain climbers in particular, there's an organization called the Korean Mountain Preservation League, consisting of a group of expatriates and Koreans who climb to pick up litter in the mountains of Korea—thereby combining a favorite hobby with a good deed. By the end of 2009, the group has removed 3,300 liters of trash and recyclables from Korea's mountains. For more information, visit the league's website at http://kmpl.org.

EugeneBell USA and EugeneBell Korea collectively make up the Eugene Bell Foundation, which has worked for over a century to provide humanitarian and developmental assistance to North Korea. EugeneBell strives primarily to bring medical treatment facilities to the North, working with donors to fight deadly diseases like tuberculosis. However, the organization also serves as a conduit for a wide spectrum of business, governmental, religious, and social organizations and individuals interested in promoting programs that benefit those in need in North Korea. Visit their website at http://www.eugenebell.org.

Finally, AeRanWon is a residential support program for pregnant and parenting women. One of its goals is to help young mothers become self-sufficient, providing housing and job training to aid these young women in moving up the income ladder. In so doing, AeRanWon helps to curb abortions in Korea—over 80 percent of the women who enroll in the program decide to keep their children. Visit them at http://aeranwon.org.

I LOVE YOU?

THE DATING GAME

Dating is a treacherous minefield wherever in the world you happen to be, and Korea certainly is no exception. This is not only a country where dating is driven by raging hormones, but also one where innate reproductive tendencies must duke it out with thousands of years' worth of theorizing about the most lucrative match, all pitted against incoming Western tendencies. What with Confucius wreaking extra havoc on the rules of the playing field, the challenge certainly is a daunting one.

Of course, boys will be boys, and girls will be, well, snobbish. Some boning up on the rudiments of Korean dating conventions may be in line for Western singles seeking love in Korea, as there are certain differences when it comes to approaching people, maintaining interest, advancing intimacy, and getting hitched. But once you are up to date with the tools of the local trade, your dating life will really just grind down to who makes you happiest overall. Just a different journey.

For those stragglers in the dating race (that's right, you in the corner, barely managing to get your *Annyeong-haseyo* out, much less moving in for the kill), the Korean Dude gives you the 411 on how to put your best foot forward and present your prime plumage, ripe for the plucking.

Q

Where are the good spots to meet singles?

I've noticed that a bar is not just a bar and a café is not just a café in Korea. In fact, there are so many different types of any given venue that I often feel I need an encyclopedia just to keep track of them. But despite the plethora of entertainment venues, I find that socializing at most places seems to be limited to the people you came with. Where can I go to meet more prospective dates, and how should I go about it?

—Hopelessly Single

A

Can the Korean Dude boast of being a master player? Perhaps not, but he may be able to offer some good options on how best to meet Korean singles.

Hopelessly Single, you are right: many Koreans do tend to flock around in their designated groups rather than branching out of their established networks. This comes thanks to extensive conditioning with group identities. By the same token, Koreans are not so receptive to random approaches by strangers, meaning that a spontaneous conversation on the subway will earn you more hates than dates. Nonetheless, there are ways to get your mingling skills back in gear.

Perhaps the most popular dating vehicle in Korea is the *sogaeting*. The term combines the words *sogae* (Korean for "introduction") and "meeting." "Meeting," in the Korean context, is understood as a practice among young Koreans—typically college students—where a group of unacquainted males and females meet with the objective of finding a suitable love interest. A group date, if you will. The practice (basically blind dating) is much more popular among adults. If you ever see two well-dressed young Koreans sitting in a café and acting very awkward around each other, they're probably on their first *sogaeting*.

If you're desperate to meet singles the fast way, you could consider a trip to booking clubs (like "meeting," this English word has been repurposed) or nightclubs. These venues practice "booking," where male clientele pay waiters to find and drag back attractive females from among the crowd present. This easy supply has its drawbacks— nightclubs cost men a pretty penny, and women will find many of the men only interested in a one-night romp. But if that's what you're looking for, to each his or her own!

You've snagged someone with potential. Now what? To call or not to call? To gift or not to gift? Can you sweet-talk without giving over power altogether? How do you keep your selection happy and engaged?

There are many aspects of dating in Korea that can either be more or less stressful for Westerners. For example, Korean lovebirds tend to adhere to the hurrying tendencies of their countrymen and seem somewhat more desensitized to the wait-to-see-who-calls-first practices of the West, where both males and females will try to wait out contacting the other as long as possible so as not to be the first to initiate contact, and thus seem more desperate. At the same time, many Korean guys and girls may expect faster commitments and greater efforts to express adoration.

Also note that Confucius (that rascal) sticks his nose even into romance. That said, one may observe many distinct characteristics about Korean men and women.

At least traditionally, Koreans in general have a particular affinity for male children. As such, while Korean girls are held to highly conservative standards by parents, boys are often spoiled just for being male—a fact attested to by several of the Dude's own Korean friends.

Also, whereas guys in the US seem more interested in sports and general displays of machismo than anything else, Korean guys seem more focused on making sure their hair is perfectly gelled. In other words, Koreans guys tend to be slightly more, ah, "metrosexual" than their Western counterparts.

Add dating tactics into the mix. American singles seem to generally abide by the "three-day" rule, a concept (immortalized by the 1996 movie *Swingers*) in which contacting a date should be done after three days have passed so as not to make the caller appear too anxious and needy. Americans also place great importance on the phrase "I love you," considered an indication of deeper commitment and only uttered to a partner when absolutely certain of its truth. All this makes for a somewhat distanced and gradual approach, where self-preservation is top priority.

It is rather amusing that Americans often have the perception that Korean girls are "gold diggers." There are certain Korean women who do require much attention and doting, perhaps since Korean girls are generally raised to be conservative and tend to be sheltered and protected by their families while growing up.

The individuals below have experienced such chaos firsthand. Perhaps their experiences may serve as a reference in your preparations.

 *Are there rules to dating a Korean dude?*

I started falling for this one Korean dude. He came from Korea just last year, but he's half-fluent in English. Communication is all right—I'm half-fluent in Korean, so we just mix the words around. We spent just about every single day with each other

during the Christmas holidays. We spent New Year's together, too, and he even got me a very expensive gift! But he has yet to ask me to be his girlfriend.

I was wondering if this not asking a girl to be your girlfriend is unusual for Korean guys. I was also wondering if there are any other unwritten "rules" regarding dating Koreans. I know this could result in harsh generalizations, but if you could answer my questions based on your experience and knowledge, that would be awesome.

—White Washed

 As you stated, generalizations are risky, but the Korean Dude can make a few general observations. At first blush, it appears your friend has yet to make up his mind, but he generally appears attracted to you. Be warned that there's also a possibility that he already assumes you two are exclusive, without having touched base with you!

Speaking strictly in terms of those dreaded generalizations, Korean guys straight from the motherland seem to have a number of key differences from their Western counterparts. Guys from Western countries seem to be much more assertive in pursuing what they desire, having been raised to be independent and outspoken. Korean guys, in contrast, seem much more accustomed to having things handed to them and are often downright clueless about how to approach girls. This

also results in them being shyer and less direct about their feelings, since they are more sensitive about their emotions, especially if they don't have much dating experience. This can be good and bad.

On the flip side, many Korean men, true to Korean fashion, are impatient and want to seal the deal ASAP. So the initial onslaught can be quite strong. Men may indulge their target

with many pleasures, such as gifts and frequent calls and text messages. Once men feel they have won you over, however, their behavior begins to change, and the emphasis seems to switch to the female working to make the male happy. At this stage, Korean men can often come off as being downright chauvinistic.

In any case, Dr. Dude would prescribe a little patience. Hang out with him some more, and if he doesn't do anything sketchy, such as chasing other girls, he may come around to confessing his true feelings.

 *Why do I have to treat strangers like family?*

I'm really confused when it comes to addressing strangers with familial terms. An *oppa* is the older brother of a woman, but I hear girlfriends calling their boyfriends *oppa* in Korean movies. Also, some good male friends of mine insist that I should call them *oppa*. Is that okay? Who can you call *oppa*?

—Wary DongSaeng

It is assumed that appellations like *eonni* and *oppa* originated in the 20th century. At that time, they were only used between family members. In Korean universities, underclassmen usually called their seniors *seonbae* or *seonbaenim* (terms for

referring to your seniors in age and grade). Soon, the familial classification moved over to the dating culture among younger women and older men, and women started calling their boyfriend *oppa*.

These days, women generally refer to close male friends and relatives as *oppa*—the now apparently multipurpose word can mean "boyfriend," "husband," or "older male friend." In a sense, calling someone "*oppa*" may give him a sense of empowerment, since you are appointing him as a kind of guardian to you. He's the "older brother" now, and what do older brothers do? Become the authority who takes care of younger sisters. On a related note, some Korean women nowadays hesitate to refer to male friends or boyfriends as *oppa* because they feel it can give undue authority or power to them.

So it's up to you whom you want to call *oppa*. If the other person is someone you are friendly with and trust, there shouldn't be much harm in adding the diminutive. But if you don't know someone quite as well or don't want to give a man the upper hand, don't call him *oppa* (even though men love to hear it from you). Just call him by his full name followed by *ssi* (like *Kim Cheolsu-ssi* for Kim Cheolsu) instead.

 **Q** *Is he just not that into me, or should I call him?*

I am a *Miguk* (American) female, and I've gone out with this one Korean dude several times. I have not heard from him in a couple of weeks. Should I write him off as uninterested, or should I call him? He usually calls me, and I don't know if Korean men expect to be the one to call and make the dates or what.

—Desperate Loveholic

 **A** A couple of weeks? The Dude hates to be harsh, but he thinks your answer is clear. No guy—Korean, American, or Zimbabwean—is going to wait weeks to call a girl if he is interested in maintaining a relationship with her. If you're not ready to give up just yet, it is possible that he has been unavoidably detained by something pressing, but he could at least have given you a preemptive heads up.

Before you give him the benefit of the doubt, you may want to answer a few questions for yourself about what you two had. How and where did you two meet? (Book club = good. Booking club = bad.) What did you usually do on your dates? (Cinecity

to watch *American Beauty* = good. DVD room to watch *American Pie* = bad.) When did he usually call you? (During lunch to "just say hi" = good. At 2 a.m. "just to drop by" = very bad.) Perhaps evaluating how much affection and respect he had for you when you were going steady may be a good gauge of his intentions.

Not surprisingly, love games are ubiquitous to Y chromosomes all over the world—all men seem to find their prey less tantalizing once acquired. By the same token, men will doggedly pursue their heart's (or hormones') desire until it is conquered. In conclusion, Korean men tend to think that they should contact a woman first. Accordingly, you would probably be better off not calling him, even though taking action may seem the preferable option. If he likes you enough to follow the trail, he'll call you.

Q *What gifts would appeal to a Korean girl?*

I recently started dating a Korean girl. These days, Korean couples do a lot of things that we don't do in North America—things like promise rings, mini-anniversaries, and matching shirts. So besides giving her my attention, love, support, and flowers, what other things should I be thinking about?

—Hungry to Please

A

The Korean Dude just consulted his female colleague about your question. She said that there is a lot of room for flexibility here depending on the woman you're dating, so the important thing is not to generalize. But if you want to try those quirky things Koreans do, get a calendar, as there is an infinite number of "days" you can keep (see "Family day elsewhere = couples' day in Korea?!"). Then add to that the main staples of birthdays and Christmas. But rather than dishing out for everything you hear Koreans do, think quality, not quantity. Also, I suggest you talk to your girlfriend about what she wants—but be slick about it. No girl wants to know what she's getting; she wants you to surprise her.

There are several "traditional" gifts that Korean couples seem to enjoy. You mentioned promise rings, referred to as

"couple rings" in Korea. Among Western couples, promise rings signify a great commitment and are not lightly given to one's heart's desire. At the same time, they don't seem to be as critical in declaring commitment among couples, although they do tend to be very expensive. "Couple Ts" are similar to couple rings—both halves of a couple are expected to wear complementary tops.

The hundred-day anniversary is just one of the possible mini-anniversaries a couple can celebrate together. (Obviously, you also have the one-month and six-month landmarks.) This has some connection with the customary Korean practice of celebrating a baby's 100th birthday to bless it for having survived its difficult first few months of life.

Notice the common thread running through the aforementioned is the intention to declare couplehood to the entire world. Koreans are big on appearances, so if you want to get creative with your "events," you have an endless range of possibilities to choose from, including flashing a message on the stadium scoreboard or singing for your lady on stage before a roomful of patrons.

In the end, however, just remember the most important things are attention, love, and support—the things you already talked about. The rest is incidental. Good luck.

You've made the calls, you've given the gifts. But how to initiate increased intimacy? The attitudes of Korean society toward sex are varied and often downright hypocritical, where judgments based on a traditional emphasis on chastity can be made by the very individuals who spur the thriving adult entertainment industry.

This is by no means to say that sex should be rushed into and openly indulged in, particularly if you are seeking a relationship with a Korean. Note that even the law sometimes does not account for all of society's subtleties, and that social perceptions may indeed take precedence over written mandates.

Q *How old do you have to be to have sex?*

I've just finished watching Park Chul-soo's *Green Chair*. The premise of the film is that an older woman (around 32) has been prosecuted for having sex with an underage man (around 19). Never mind whether these are Korean ages or Western ages—I'm confused by a piece of information I read on the website of the International Gay and Lesbian Association suggesting that the age of consent is 13. So either the info on the website is wrong, or the premise of the film is flawed. Can you clarify?

—A Befuddled Snake

A According to the Criminal Code, a person may be charged with rape if they have sex with someone under 13. But that doesn't mean it's all right to have sex with someone over 13 when that person is not considered an adult. The Dude has never heard of teenagers being arrested for having sex with one another. But it would be a different story if an adult had sex with a minor, since this society considers them too immature to make crucial decisions. In the long run, the court (the Dude guesses) will make its decision based on all the circumstances in the case. There are many other laws concerning adolescents. The Adolescent Protection Act, for example, stipulates that those 19 and under are minors. For your reference, the Civil Code says that males over 18 and females over 16 are free to get married without their parents' consent.

 Sex aside, there are many occasions for increasing intimacy between you and your partner. In Korea, there seems to be a wealth of days dedicated to the celebration of love and couplehood. If nothing else, these days certainly help to break out of the routine and keep the love coming (mostly in material form).

Do note that there are Korean "love holidays" and adapted Western holidays to consider for couple celebrations. You may find it wise to pull out a calendar before studying the following.

Q *Family day elsewhere = couples' day in Korea?!*

I've noticed that several Western holidays have been carried over to Korea. But am I incorrect in observing that many of them are regarded and celebrated a touch differently from in the US? What are the different modern holidays in Korea, and how do I celebrate them?

—Love Day Enthusiast

A There are several Western holidays that have been carried over to Korea. Several have acquired somewhat different purposes from the original.

Let's begin with what the Korean Dude refers to as the "14 Series." They commence with the international love holiday of Valentine's Day. There's a twist, though: in Korea and Japan, women present chocolate gifts to their men. Men don't reciprocate until March 14, or White Day, which was created by confectionery companies looking to boost revenue. On the next page, you can find a quick chart showing the (largely self-explanatory) days to remember, including one non-14th day.

Unlike in the Western world, Christmas is mostly spent outside the home with significant others (or friends, for singles). As such, many of the hip areas turn into veritable sardine cans.

Meanwhile, New Year's Day, while generally celebrated in the West with that special New Year's love kiss, is largely a family day, replete with visits to extended family and *jesa* rites to honor ancestors.

"14 Day"	Date	How to Celebrate	Popularity
Diary Day	Jan. 14	Couples exchange their plans for the year.	Lukewarm
Valentine's Day	Feb. 14	Women give chocolates to men.	High
White Day	Mar. 14	Men give candies to women.	High
Black Day	Apr. 14	Singles mourn their singledom by eating *jjajangmyeon* (noodles w/ black bean sauce) .	Moderate
Rose Day	May 14	Lovers buy each other roses.	Lukewarm
Kiss Day	June 14	Couples exchange kisses—either of the osculatory or Hershey's variety.	Lukewarm
Ring/Silver Day	July 14	Couples exchange rings.	Lukewarm
Green Day	Aug. 14	Couples walk in the woods to escape the heat.	Lukewarm
Music Day	Sept. 14	Couples exchange CDs and/or enjoy music together.	Lukewarm
Wine Day	Oct. 14	Couples enjoy wine.	Lukewarm
Movie Day	Nov. 14	Couples watch a movie together.	Lukewarm
Hug Day	Dec. 14	Couples exchange hugs.	Lukewarm
Pepero Day	Nov. 11	Couples exchange *Pepero*, a famous Korean treat consisting of a long cracker covered in chocolate (said to resemble the "one"s in the date November 11, or 1111 in numbers).	High

HAVING A MERRY KOREAN CHRISTMAS: YULETIDE KOREAN-STYLE MEANS ROMANCE AND FUN

BY JISU AHN

Christmas season never fails to bring hope and joy to the hearts of people. Korea is no different from other countries when it comes to the romanticism that goes along with the snowy season. Christmas trees and images of Santa Claus liven up the streets in Korea, while Christmas carols can be heard in all the shops.

Although the spirit of Christmas is present among Koreans, Korea's cultural background means that the way people view and celebrate Christmas in a somewhat different way from the Christian West. In countries where Christianity is the main religion, people celebrate the birth of Jesus Christ by going to church, recreating nativity scenes, and spending time with their families.

Since large parts of the Korean population have no religious affiliation (46 percent) or follow the Buddhist tradition (26 percent), Christmas in Korea is more secular. Few people regard it as a religious celebration; rather, they enjoy it as a day to celebrate the end of the year. You will find many Christmas trees and images of Santa Claus on the streets, but you will not see many nativity scenes, which are very common in Christian countries.

Unlike in Western countries where Christmas is a family holiday, it is seen in Korea a day to celebrate with your significant other as a couple. So while people in other countries get stressed during Christmas season about facing family members, Koreans get stressed about finding a date for Christmas Eve. Those who have a special person with whom to spend Christmas often enjoy romantic dinners and go to places in downtown Seoul like Gwanghwamun and Myeong-dong, where they can enjoy the beautiful spectacle of Christmas lights and decorations.

Those who fail to get a date for Christmas spend it with friends. Fortunately, the last days of December see many year-end parties, or *songnyeonhoe*, where Koreans gather together to celebrate the end of the year. *Songnyeonhoe* are usually held among old classmates, co-workers, and other social groups and are characterized by lots of eating and drinking, as well as an overall atmosphere of unrestrained celebration.

Meanwhile, Christmas shopping in Korea is not as frantic as in Western countries. Sales do increase at the end of the year, but gift shopping is not a big problem, since it is not customary to exchange presents with family members or friends for Christmas. Usually, Koreans will just buy presents for their significant other.

Although Christmas is celebrated differently in Korea from other countries, the overall sense of hope and optimism that comes along with the season is not lost. The Korean spirit of Christmas is alive, and you can enjoy it if you know the right places to go. If you want to have a taste of Christmas, you can visit the various theme parks, where the Christmas spirit is already in evidence. Lotte World currently holds two "Happy Christmas Parades" a day, as well as an onstage musical performance called *Cinderella's Christmas Party*. You can enjoy all the Christmas dancing and singing for an entrance fee of 25,000 won. Lotte World is located at Jamsil Station, Lines 2 and 8. For more information, call (02) 411-2000 or visit http://www.lotteworld.com. Everland has also prepared its own annual festival, "Christmas Fantasy." You can also enjoy a beautiful parade and fireworks display with an entrance fee of 33,000 won. For more information, call (031) 320-5000 or visit http://www.everland.com.

If you want to have fun at a more reasonable price, you can visit Seoul Plaza in front of City Hall, where a skating rink is open from mid-December to mid-February. The entrance fee, which includes skates and a helmet, is only 1,000 won per person. The rink is open 12 hours a day starting at 10:00 a.m.

In the area around Seoul Plaza, you can enjoy not only the beautiful lights of Cheonggyecheon Stream but also the luminarie, which according to government officials is currently being planned. For a more religious Christmas experience, you can visit Myeong-dong Cathedral, where there are masses all day long on Christmas as well as one on Christmas Eve. Myeong-dong Cathedral is located at Exits 5 and 8, Myeong-dong Station, Line 4. For more information, call (02) 774-1784, or visit http://www.mdsd.or.kr.

2 TYING THE KNOT

Why are Koreans so obsessed with weddings? The question may be like asking why dogs bark, why cats meow, or why Koreans love kimchi. It's just built into their genetics—after thousands of years of evolution and environmental conditioning, it's immutable and absolute.

Just kidding. The Dude wouldn't ever leave you with a "that's just the way things are" answer, right? But I do hope you come away with an idea of how big a part marriage plays in Korean society. Of course, any country's inhabitants spend a fair amount of time thinking about and planning marriage. But there is an especial candor about marriage in Korea, where people won't hesitate to ask if you are married, or planning to get married, and will comment on whether you are marriage material—even to individuals barely over the age of 20. In fact, many young Koreans fresh out of college will immediately begin to worry about whether they can find suitable spouse material, and soon.

Be warned that Korean weddings stretch far beyond simply a day for the couple. Much emphasis is placed on marriage ceremonies as a depiction of the honor brought to two families based on the matrimonial union, as well as social status and wealth based on the grandeur of the wedding. Because of this, weddings tend to be very high-profile affairs, with the invitee list including not only close friends and family but also acquaintances and colleagues of both parents and the couple.

For the humble Westerner who has always dreamed of a small yet beautiful, romantic, and unique wedding ceremony this pomp and circumstance may be simultaneously alarming, overwhelming, and, perhaps, disappointing. But think of it optimistically, and the entire affair may turn out to be surprisingly intriguing—and entertaining.

 *What are Korean weddings like?*

A good Korean friend of mine recently asked me to attend his wedding. I happily accepted, but having never been to a Korean wedding, I'm both curious and a bit nervous to go. Are Korean weddings still very traditionally performed? Or are they very flamboyant affairs? And am I expected to do anything?

—Novice GUEST

Most Koreans today get married in ceremonies that combine Western and Korean elements. Many couples opt to jump the broom at wedding halls built specifically to facilitate wedding planning and large numbers of guests. Typically, the quasi-Western part of the ceremony comes first.

There are a few differences from most Western weddings in this portion, however. For example, there is no real superstition about the groom seeing the bride in her wedding dress before the ceremony, like you find in Western countries. Indeed, couples generally stay together for the entire day, getting their makeup and hair done together and greeting their guests as

they arrive. Also, whereas gifts for Western weddings are typically handled by wedding registries, many guests at Korean weddings will bring envelopes of money. Colleagues and friends of the couple will often pool money together to purchase one grand present. After, and often during, the ceremony, guests are usually offered a buffet or three-course meal. Wedding parties don't usually continue late into the night.

For the traditional part of the wedding, the couple changes into traditional wedding *hanbok* clothing and goes behind a table (called a *choryesang*) in an area set off by a decorative screen, where they bow to each other and take a seat. The highlight of the ceremony is the sharing of a special white wine, called *jeongjong*, which traditionally was poured into cups made from the two halves of a gourd grown by the bride's mother. The bride and groom sip from their separate cups, after which the wine is mixed together, repoured into the cups, and sipped again as a part of the wedding vow, or *keunbaerye*. After this is the *pyebaek* ceremony, in which the bride offers her new in-laws jujubes and chestnuts (symbols of children). They, in turn, offer her tea. At the ceremony's conclusion, the parents toss the dates and chestnuts at the bride, and the couple tries together to catch the food in her skirt. Finally, the groom gives his mother and new bride piggyback rides, symbolizing him supporting them both.

When it comes to Korean weddings, you can't forget the *ham* processions that take place the night before the ceremony. In the *ham* processions, gifts of fabrics, jewelry, and money are passed back and forth between the new in-laws. From the home of the groom's family, friends of his set off wearing masks of dried squid and carrying the boxes of gifts. Together, they walk to the home of the bride's family, chanting, "*Ham* for sale, buy a *ham*." In this way, they announce the impending union to the neighborhood. On the way, neighbors who see the procession will often sing and dance with the participants. Meanwhile, the bride's home is decorated with ornamental room dividers and a table of food, usually including *sirutteok* (a rice cake with ground red beans). The *ham* boxes often include contractual documents having to do with the wedding. The bride's father will review these documents and (depending on the individual traditions of the family) give the *sirutteok* to the bride and the other people present in—but not visiting—her home. With the rest of the gifts, the bride's family will often take out a portion and send the remainder back to the groom's home, concluding the friendly exchange.

 ## Who pays for the wedding and why?

One of my Korean friends who is about to get married told me some interesting things about the deal she's getting. Korean in-laws usually provide a house or deposit (although her fiancé

is a firstborn son, and she has to move into that family unit). But the Korean couple has to pay for the wedding themselves. Now, I find the next bit interesting: she doesn't get to keep the wedding gifts (cash, basically). It goes to the parents. I do gather that it's the parents who are most honored at a Korean wedding. She says it's "help money" to cover the expenses. But she just told me that she and hubby pay for the wedding. Do they borrow from the parents and pay them back in gift money? Is the gift money enough to leave anything for buying house things? What is the real deal for Korean newlyweds?

—Fiscal Inquirer

In traditional Confucian Korean society, children are regarded as dependent on their parents. Though this bond between parents and children has weakened in modern Korea, a person is still considered to be part of a family unit rather than an individual. So marriage is, in many cases, regarded as a union between "two families" rather than between "a man and a woman."

In weddings, parents who are honored, not more than as the bride and groom. Middle-aged people generally regard their children as mature and independent only after they get married. So it is also the parents' duty to find a good match for their offspring, and the majority of the guests were probably invited by the parents anyway.

The ratio of wedding costs paid by the parents and the

couple differs from family by family. In some cases, one side—parents or children—may opt to pay the entire cost. But weddings are often too expensive for the young couple to cover, so they have to depend on their parents. In general, Korean parents pay for most of the wedding, as well as the house, furniture, and home appliances, and they take the cash collected at the wedding as a way of recouping these expenses. Whether parents end up in the black or in the red depends on how many guests attend to celebrate the event, as well as how many give cash gifts.

Koreans are not so strict in calculating money between family members. Even if the cash gifts do not cover the wedding costs, the newlyweds don't come under any obligation to repay their parents for the deficit. Instead, the newlyweds (especially when the groom is the first son) are expected to live with their parents, who support them. This tradition in parent/child relationships has been changing and does not apply in all cases. But the fundamental rule doesn't seem to have disappeared yet.

MARRIAGE À LA KOREA

BY RICHARD HARRIS

Lights! Camera! Action! This isn't Hollywood, but a wedding—à la Korea. I got married to a Korean woman and went through one of the great rites of passage in this country: marriage. Here is my experience.

To be honest, I was as apprehensive about getting married in Korea as I was excited. After all, who wouldn't be curious to know what it's like getting hitched under the bright lights and close scrutiny of hundreds of spectators, camerapeople, and a cadre of waitresses and waiters, along with the random few who always seem to wander in at the most inopportune times? All this while a cacophony of cell phones goes off in the background.

At most Korean weddings (including my own), the groom welcomes guests at the entrance before the ceremony starts, while the bride sits in a tiny side room greeting visitors, having her picture taken with loved ones, and continually having her makeup attended to by her *doumi*, or "helper."

When the big moment arrives, a *sahoeja* (a master of ceremonies) talks everyone through the event as the mothers of the bride and groom walk down the aisle together, light their respective candles on the stage, and bow to each other. After that, they take a front-row seat beside their husband (or, as was the case at my wedding, my cousin, who filled in for my late father). It is then that the groom walks down the aisle, followed shortly thereafter by the bride and her father, who stroll down the carpet arm in arm, just as it's done in the West.

For the next then minutes, a *jurye* (usually a respected, older academic figure, but in our case a hired gentleman whom we met for the first time only 30 minutes before the ceremony) extols the virtues of marriage and love, along with the responsibilities each partner must shoulder during the union. Once the *jurye's* speech was done, we lit a candle onstage, popped open a bottle of champagne, and cut the ceremonial cake. That's when the bowing took place. We walked over to my bride's parents, and I made a split-second decision. Instead of giving the traditional *banjeol* (standing half-bow), I went further by giving a *keunjeol* (a kneeling bow reserved for ceremonious occasions) to my parents-in-law. This was met with shrieks of laughter from our guests and a combination of surprise, respect, and mortification on my wife's side. After that, my bride and I shuffled over to my mother and cousin, giving them a traditional standing bow before walking back up the aisle under a shower of confetti and other party tricks. After the wedding ceremony, we socialized, took pictures, and moved on to a restaurant for a reception that fused the best of Western traditions (the speeches and the long meal) with the best of Korean traditions (no one gets out alive?).

For years prior, I had denied that I would ever get married in Korea that way. It just seemed so tacky, with all the noise and light pollution and streamers falling from the ceiling. It's hard to say what exactly turned me onto the road to acceptance. Was it love? Compromise? Maybe it was a little of everything. But in the end, our wedding was a celebration of love and a party of the highest order. People cried and rejoiced. And when all was said and done, two kids who had fallen for each other with the simple line, "Do you have a light, by any chance?" formalized one of the world's most longstanding traditions.

We tied the knot.

We got hitched.

We got married in Korea, confetti and all.

Q
What are Koreans' attitudes toward interracial marriage?

I've noticed these days that there are more and more international couples, where one half of the couple is Korean and the other half Caucasian or some other ethnicity. From what I understand, Koreans do not have a particularly high opinion of such relationships—or, at least, they haven't traditionally. I wanted to know what exactly the current attitude and reaction toward interracial marriages is.

—Madam Mix-a-Lot

The Korean Dude cannot lie and say that society is completely accepting of interracial marriages. However, he can confidently state that attitudes have become much improved over the past few years.

Though information on attitudes about interracial marriage is hard to come by and generalize from, surveys have found most respondents these days showing favorable opinions toward mixed marriages. Statistics have shown a significant number of interracial marriages taking place every year in Korea. National Statistical Office figures in 2010 indicated that over 34,000 marriages (roughly equal to 10 out of every 100 couples) were between Koreans and partners of different ethnicities. Similar numbers have kept up in recent years, contributing to the booming international presence in the country and highlighting the need for measures to support non-Korean spouses in their integration into Korean society.

Efforts at the local and central government levels have been focused on this goal, with government ministries such as the Ministry of Health, Welfare and Family Affairs taking a leading role in education programs, providing instruction in the Korean language and culture, and offering other programs to assist with child care and counseling services. With this trend of increasing numbers of mixed marriages, and with measures in place to assist the transition to a more multicultural society, interracial marriages are becoming an established and valued part of a country that has traditionally been quite ethnically homogeneous.

LOVE IS GRAND BUT NOT EASY

BY RICHARD STANSFIELD

A lot of things have changed since I first came to Korea in 1996. For one thing, there weren't as many Valentine's Day spinoffs as there are now. Another is that there are more mixed couples (composed of a Korean and a foreigner) than before. Back in 1996, it was viewed as very unacceptable for a foreign man to date a Korean woman.

There's still some residual resistance. My parents are from different countries, and my students sometimes remark, "Your grandparents must have been opposed to the marriage." They are surprised when I say, "No, it was never an issue with them." To them, it's a given that the parents would be opposed simply because their child's fiancé was from another country.

Statistics from countries like Canada, where mixed marriages are common, show that divorce rates among such couples are not much higher than among "traditional" couples. My parents still have a good marriage, and I know that the most important ingredient to their success has been communication. Therein lies the rub when talking about Korean/foreign couples. Every year, some 1,500 Americans marry Korean women, and a staggering 80 percent of those marriages end in divorce. To try to alleviate this problem, groups like the USO have offered "marriage courses" for mixed couples.

In one lesson, Arthur and Sue Kinsler, a mixed couple, act out a problem that they have encountered—and, judging from the reactions of the couples watching, a common one. Arthur asks his wife, "What's wrong?" Sue stays silent, looking down with arms crossed over her chest. Arthur continues, "If I did something wrong, you've got to tell me what." Sue continues her silence, even turning her body so that she's facing away from him. Arthur persists: "Tell your husband what you're feeling." Finally, in frustration, he jumps up in the air: "*TALK TO ME!*"

It's a story I've heard time and time again from foreign men who've had Korean girlfriends: "She doesn't communicate." Sue tries to explain that Korean women don't feel confident about their English (that is, their ability to communicate things precisely), so they choose to bottle up their feelings instead. Harboring negative feelings and becoming ever more embittered is referred to in Korea as *han*. The flip side of this comes with the explosive displays that occur when these long-repressed emotions finally boil to the surface. To a Westerner, these outbursts can be confusing and frightening.

Sue adds that Koreans feel discouraged from talking if they feel their partner lacks *nunchi*. *Nunchi* is one of those culture-specific words that are difficult to explain. Literally meaning "eye-measure," it refers to picking up on another person's mood from subtle signals—kind of like "feeling a vibe."

Related to *nunchi* is *gibun*, another concept that is difficult to explain. It's often translated as "mood," as in "He's in a good mood today." But a *gibun* is more easily upset than a mood. I might get into a bad mood if someone yells at me, but my *gibun* might be put into disequilibrium if someone who's yelled at me in the past so much as enters the room.

I know from my lifelong experience and knowledge of mixed marriages that lack of communication is the surest way to destroy a relationship—any relationship, but especially a mixed one. Another thing that my parents' marriage has taught me is that being willing to be less stubborn and more compromising is especially important for a successful mixed marriage. Unfortunately, it seems that many in Korea learn these lessons too late, after the breakup. With increased contact between the different cultures, we all hope for a commensurate increase in understanding and decrease in the amount of heartache.

DEBATE ON THE FUTURE OF KOREAN IDENTITY

BY ROBERT KOEHLER

International marriage and *honhyeorin* (literally, "mixed-blood people") are not exactly recent phenomena in Korea. For ages, foreigners have been visiting Korea (not always with invitations), with some of them putting down roots and making their contribution to the gene pool. During the later Goryeo era, even Korea's kings were married off to Mongolian princesses under the watchful eye of China's Yuan Dynasty. It's presumed that at least some of the Arab and Persian traders who came to Korea in years past stayed, took local wives, and eventually blended into the population at large. And, of course, more than a few Japanese took Korean husbands and wives during the colonial era, starting with the Korean royal family.

In common parlance, however, the term *honhyeorin* (which may soon fall into disuse due to its somewhat negative connotation) refers to individuals who look distinctively of mixed-race extraction. This phenomenon, too, probably has a longer history than many might expect. For instance, the Dutchman Jan Janse Weltevree, who built cannons for the Korean king after being shipwrecked on the Korean coast in 1628, was said to have taken a Korean wife who bore him two (presumably mixed-race) children. Some suggest that fellow Dutchman Hendrik Hamel and the crew of the shipwrecked *Sperwer* went forth and procreated during their stay in Korea's southwest.

The numbers were relatively small, however, until the Korean War, when the influx of US military personnel led to what is considered the first "generation" of mixed-race Koreans, the Amerasians. They were followed in the 60s and 70s by the Lai Daihan, the children of Korean soldiers fighting in Vietnam and local women. In the 90s, as laborers from developing nations in South and Southeast Asia came to Korea in search of the "Korean Dream," marriages between them and Korean women led to the birth of the "Kosian," short for "Korean-Asian." Finally, and in the long run most significantly, recent years have witnessed a huge spike in multiracial children as a number of demographic factors have forced rural Korean men to essentially "import" Korean wives from nations like Vietnam and the Philippines.

Currently, there are some 35,000 mixed-race Koreans—5,000 Amerasians and 35,000 Kosians. This number is likely to skyrocket, however, if current demographic trends hold true. According to the National Statistical Office, some 10 percent of all marriages in 2010 were international unions. The trend was particularly acute in the countryside, where some rural counties recorded international marriage rates of over 30 percent. By the year 2020, there are expected to be some 1.67 million mixed-race Koreans—more than the current population of Gangwon-do. By that year, one in three newborns will be multiracial, as will one in five people under the age of 20.

It wouldn't be an exaggeration to say that for a society that has prided itself on its ethnic homogeneity, all this could be a shock to the system. The realization that Korea may not be a by-and-large homogenous society for much longer has sparked both reflection on the conditions faced by mixed-race Koreans, who are often the target of bullying and discrimination, and debate over what, exactly, constitutes a "Korean" national identity.

We may be seeing some changes already. According to recent media reports, over 50 percent of Koreans are now okay with marrying foreigners, a percentage that would have been unimaginable just a few years ago. When asked in a recent survey by the *Chosun Ilbo* to pick their most ideal hunk, the highest percentage of women selected Daniel Henney, an Amerasian model

Mr. Henney

and actor. You can find more and more multiracial figures on radio and TV. Perhaps most importantly, the media are no longer ignoring multiracial Koreans as if it were ashamed they even existed.

The changing social debate is being reflected in law. There is now widespread political support for, at the very least, allowing mixed-race Koreans to join the Korean military, where they were previously forbidden. The government is now pushing anti-discrimination legislation and has stopped the use of the term *honhyeorin* (with its overtones of "impurity") in official documents, replacing it with the preferred "children of international marriages." Authorities have established centers to help international couples adjust to life in Korea. They will also grant citizenship and residency rights to foreigners in non-registered common law marriages with Koreans, as well as to their children. Previously, such rights were bestowed only upon foreigners who registered their marriages and children with the civil authorities.

It's hard to know whether the sudden interest in international marriage and multiracial children will continue. But with the numbers going nowhere but up and fast, the issues are unlikely to remain quiet for very long.

3 AFTER THE BIG DAY

The big day has been planned, executed, and celebrated, with associated nerves and sorrows drowned in champagne and wine. Rings exchanged, vows declared, and new in-laws greeted, you and your spouse travel to distant lands on your official nuptial vacation. Time passes. You settle into your new home with said spouse, no longer sacrificing work curfew for a few more minutes in bed with the honey. Babies have been conceived. Babies have been born. Sleep deficiency is starting to take its toll on both emotions and physical appearance. "Can't stop me touching you" becomes "Can't you stop touching me." Long-forgotten honeymoon pictures are starting to wear around the edges.

What now? Do you still love him or her? Does he or she still love you? Is there any passion to keep the fire between you going? Is there even time to explore what emotions may be left? What keeps the constant metamorphosis from heading ineluctably into dissolution?

It's probably a conundrum that every married couple has had to face, Korean or not. Of course, Koreans have developed their own terminology for just this sort of phenomenon. Want to know more about how Koreans deal with mellowing marriages? Read ahead.

Q *What is* jeong?

I know *jeong* is a very typical emotion for Koreans. I would like to know more about it in a concrete way. What is *jeong*? Why people always say Koreans are full of *jeong*? How can we explain *jeong* in Koreans' daily life? I've done searches on it in some Korean search engines, but I couldn't find a very relevant explanation.

—Emerging Empath

In simple terms, *jeong* (情) can be described as an emotional attachment that is not necessarily platonic or romantic. For example, the relationship between husband and wife in a long marriage may be described as *jeong*, as they remain loyal and faithful to each other despite the state of their romantic and physical inclinations for each other. Linguistically speaking, *jeong* can be compared to kimchi: you have to wait until it ripens. Just as people use the expression *mas-i* (taste) *deunda* (develops over time), they also say *jeong-i deunda*.

Jeong is a fundamental basis for human relationships, and you cannot walk away from it easily once you have developed it. It is often used in relationships between lovers—people talk about your *jeong-deun nim* ("sweetheart") or *jeong-in* ("sweetheart," more formal), and about *tongjeong* (having an affair with someone). But you can also develop *jeong* for things, such as your old high school or a country you lived in.

According to Drs. Christopher K. Chung and Samson Cho of Harbor-UCLA Medical Center, the presence of *jeong* makes for a unique societal structure in Korea, where emphasis is placed on loyalty and commitment that is often lacking in logic or reason. Interactions often carry the assumption of commitment. Because commitments are based on contextual significance—rather than being contractual and defined, as with marriage in Western culture—individuals are easily integrated as members of a collective, where autonomy and individualism are diminished. In referring to themselves, many Koreans will say "our husband" or "our wife," rather than "my husband" or "my wife." In this way, the concept of "I" is weakened for the sake of strengthening *jeong*. By the same token, "we" in Korea often means "I, bonded by *jeong*, to you," whereas in English, "we" just represents any collection of "I"s.

Jeong clearly has its pros and cons. Warm, rich interpersonal relationships come as a result of it, but what should be objective decisions—for example, those made in the political and professional arenas—can often be based on *jeong* instead. Also, when connections formed through *jeong* are betrayed, *han* (恨) can develop. The theologian Suh Nam-dong describes *han* as a "feeling of unresolved resentment against injustices suffered, a sense of helplessness because of the overwhelming odds against one, a feeling of acute pain in one's guts and bowels, making the whole body writhe and squirm,

and an obstinate urge to take revenge and to right the wrong—all these combined."

Both *jeong* and *han* seem to derive from the passionate nature of many Koreans. Once *jeong* is established, they pour their hearts into their relationships and will only (if ever) break a friendship under very extenuating circumstances. By the same token, once *han* develops, it is near impossible to resolve.

 *In marriage:* jeong *or love?*

This question may seem disrespectful to some Koreans, but I'm genuinely curious, and I don't know where to find a reliable answer. Please help me if you can.

I meet many Koreans who say that they "don't love" their husband or wife but that they have "good *jeong*" with them. They seem to be satisfied with having good *jeong*. I also strongly suspect that many of those with good *jeong* but not love are sexually promiscuous, or at least unfaithful to their spouse. How common is infidelity in South Korea? How socially acceptable is it? How socially acceptable is it to have good *jeong* with your spouse instead of love? Has any research been done on love vs. *jeong*, or on infidelity?

A *Jeong* surely functions in the relationship between husbands and wives, who unwittingly take *jeong* for children, or any other reason, as an excuse for staying in wedlock. It's true that Korea used to be, and still, is one of those nations where people put family and home before love.

Probably in the same context, the infidelity rate in Korea has recently been going up. Shockwaves rippled through the country when a 2005 survey of housewives in their 20s and

30s showed some 25 percent of them to be involved in serious extramarital affairs. Of course, husbands are pretty much expected to be unfaithful—not surprising, given the stunning number of adult entertainment venues that men claim they are forced to indulge in by domineering work superiors.

An interesting fact is that only 5.1 percent of the aforementioned cheating housewives would consider an actual divorce. So it looks like love (and love affairs) and marriage are two different things to some Koreans, judging solely from these statistics.

If we look at the matter from a general perspective, we can say that Koreans know that passionate love will not last as long as marriage. Also, when people say they are in *jeong* but not in love, you have to consider that some of them mean it literally, while others say it as an expression of love.

In general, Koreans are not as forthright as Westerners when they talk about love: while young couples may be quick to say, "I love you," many Koreans seem stuck in a rut when it comes to actually discussing a relationship or affection once puppy love has passed (although many are becoming more direct and straightforward these days). However, one thing the Dude can say for sure is that with the infidelity rate going up, more and more Koreans are likely to ask themselves the question you've just asked: "Is *jeong* enough?"

CULTURE SHOCK

1 FOREVERMORE QUIRKY

We promised we would turn "cultural quirk into quick cultural understanding." But the things gathered in this section are elements that may very well remain cultural quirks—and often quite endearing ones at that. (Other elements, of course, are meant more to ensure that you stay at the top of your game in social situations.)

As a quick introduction, here is a list of some common social taboos and general no-nos in Korea, some more eccentric or innocuous than others:

- People's names should not be written in red ink. In fact, extensive use of red ink should be avoided in general.
- Whistling at night is not encouraged, as it may attract ghosts.
- When you are visiting somebody's home, it is not considered particularly polite to turn up empty-handed. A simple gift, such as fruit or cake, is always welcome.
- When entering somebody's home, always remove your shoes. This also applies to some restaurants. The shoes and the change in floor level at the entrance should usually indicate what to do.
- It is considered rude to smoke in front of elders or seniors—unless they initiate it.
- When giving or receiving objects of any kind, you should use two hands. The left hand, in particular, should never be used alone to give or receive something.
- Don't ask your girlfriend or boyfriend to eat chicken wings. If you do, they will fly away. Same with shoes: if you gift your lover with shoes, they will put them on and run away.
- Pregnant women are not encouraged to eat chicken. If they do, it is believed they will give birth to babies with chicken skin.

At the Table . . .

- When sitting down for a meal, younger diners should not take up their chopsticks or begin eating before their elders have done so.
- Chopsticks should not be planted upright in a bowl of rice or other food. They should always be laid down next to the bowl or plate.
- When pouring or receiving glasses of an alcoholic beverage, you should always use two hands in front of somebody of senior status. When drinking from a glass poured by somebody senior, you should

turn your upper body to the side, indicating respect.

- It is considered impolite to whistle or sing at the table.
- Koreans in their 30s or older do not usually go Dutch when eating or drinking together. Common practice is for one person to pay the bill, and that person is usually the most senior person present—although the custom is now being oriented toward taking turns at paying.

Many of the conditions above can be explained with reference to Confucianism—for example, the customs of waiting for elders to begin eating during mealtimes and using two hands to pour drinks for and hand objects to older people are quite clearly intended as signs of deference to seniors. Such conspicuous gestures show that juniors are not relaxing or treating their interaction with someone older as something unimportant. Similarly, the practice of paying for the meals of those younger than oneself can also be seen as adhering to Confucian practices, as those older in society are entrusted with caring for their subordinates. Meanwhile, inserting chopsticks upright into food is frowned upon because it is something done during a Confucian *jesa* rite in commemoration of deceased ancestors, and is therefore loaded with too much symbolic value and connotations of death. Red ink is generally used to record the names of deceased persons in family registers and on funeral banners to drive off evil spirits—hence, once again, an association with death.

To provide some elucidation about this aspect of Korean culture:

Q *Just how confucian is Korea?*

I've heard it said that Korea is the most Confucian country in the world. I'm not very familiar with the theology behind Confucianism, so I was wondering what exactly a Confucian society is and what this means?

—Befuddled by Confucius

A Confucianism is not a theistic religion. It can be better described as an ethical and philosophical system aimed at producing a harmonious, just, and smoothly functioning state and society. In its traditional form, it placed emphasis on personal education and improvement through mastering classic Chinese literary works and composition in order to become fit to serve and help administer the state. Young Korean men would take part in highly competitive civil service examinations to reach such positions of power.

Confucianism arrived on the Korean Peninsula as early as the Three Kingdoms Period (57 BC–AD 668), and its principles were gradually adopted by successive Korean kingdoms and dynasties for the administering of the state. In fact, Korea began to adhere so strictly to the ideals of Confucius that even the Chinese were said to have regarded the Korean adherents as more virtuous and to have called Korea "the country of

Eastern decorum."

Neo-Confucianism, based on the thought of Song Dynasty scholar Zhu Xi, was strongly endorsed as a basis for national governance and social relations in the Joseon Dynasty (1392–1910).

What this means for Korean society today is that many elements of Confucian thought—ritual, relationships, filial piety, and so on—still influence the actions of individuals and groups. Confucian hierarchical relationships, in particular, are extremely important. These include the relationships between ruler and subject; father and son; husband and wife; older brother and younger brother; and friend and friend.

Returning to the list at the beginning of this subsection, there are also elements that are based more on common sense (although this isn't to say Confucian principles are nonsensical). Removing shoes, for one, has more to do with Korea's floor-sitting culture—which in turn is based on the system of *ondol* floor heating during colder weather—than with anything philosophically based. Of course, since shoes carry the dirt of the outdoors, it's also more sanitary for individuals to remove theirs before entering the home.

Of course, the remainder—such as those having to do with chicken wings and chicken skin—are, quite clearly, "mild" superstitions: not fervently believed, but kept in mind just in case they contain an element of truth. Here are some more:

 **Q** *Where'd the fourth floor go?*

I've noticed that a lot of office and residential buildings in Korea don't have a fourth floor. What is the reason for this? Is the number four bad luck, and what, if any, traditional beliefs are behind it?

—Stuck on a Missing Floor

 **A** The explanation is actually simple. The Sino-Korean character for death, *sa* (死), is pronounced the same as the number four. You would think that people today wouldn't consider the phonetic connection all that important. But traditional practices die hard. There are, however, several buildings that replace the number "4" with a seemingly incongruous "F."

 *Fan death?*

Every summer, I've read about mysterious deaths attributed to people using fans in a room with the door and windows shut. But I have just returned from a meeting with my colleagues from 18 other Asian countries and discovered that no other country in Asia has "fan deaths." Do you have any theories as to why this phenomenon is unique to Korea?

—Fan of Fans

 This is an urban legend, and it seems like the news media are to blame for its perpetuation, eager as they are to publish inaccurate stories reeking with sensationalism to a public equally eager to consume it. A few years ago, a *JoongAng Daily* article titled "Newspapers Fan Belief in Urban Myth" attempted to debunk the death-by-fanning legend. In the story, a coroner responsible for performing autopsies on many victims this so-called "fan death" phenomenon is quoted as saying, "We really can't apply hypothermia to fan accidents. I found that most of the victims already had some condition like heart disease or serious alcoholism."

The premise of this commonly held belief is that if an electric fan is running in a sealed room, its action will lower

body temperature to hypothermic levels. But this hypothermia hypothesis is unlikely because fans are only really used during the humid summer months and would just blow a lot of hot air around—if anything, they would cause heat stroke.

Others claim that the action of the fans depletes the oxygen in the room, causing carbon dioxide to build up in its stead and sink to the ground (where you sleep) to suffocate you. But most rooms aren't completely sealed, and the fan would do more to mix the carbon dioxide with the air than to separate them.

Another conjecture floating around is that the airflow passing over your face somehow creates an anomalous vacuum in the front of your mouth and nose cavity. I'm happy to report that I've tried this one myself and survived with nothing more than cottonmouth and a dry throat—probably from breathing in the dust from the fan rotors. It's about time to pull the plug on this fan fable.

Q *What are the national traits of Koreans?*

—PIQUED

Koreans are often referred to as the "Italians of the East," as both ethnicities exhibit a fiery, passionate nature with a particular penchant for food, family, song, and romance. Such elements explain the popularity of *hallyu*, or the "Korean Wave"—cultural exports that reflect Koreans and their universally appealing preferences.

In evaluating the nature of Koreans, one cannot ignore their fervent patriotism. Considering Korea's history, such a small country would have had a very difficult time surviving as long as it has without a nationalistic spirit. Throughout its days, Korea has been met with constant onslaughts from the outside—serving as a tributary state to both the Mongols and Qing China during the Goryeo and Joseon periods, and repeatedly fending off invasions from Japan. A distrust of foreign culture stemming from this history even led the Regent Heungseon Daewongun (1821–1898) to close the nation off to all foreign trade and communication, earning Korea the nickname of "Hermit Kingdom." However, Korean pride truly blossomed during the Japanese occupation (officially between 1910 and 1945). Lamenting the loss of their culture during this difficult period, Koreans grew very protective of their country and began making efforts to declare their cultural identity. It was during this time that the Korean flag, the Taegeukgi, was created, and that the "Aegukga" was first adopted as the Korean national anthem. The national pride has remained among today's Korean youth, as was especially apparent during the 2002 World Cup, when hordes of Koreans from all over the country flocked to the streets to cheer for the national team.

Another quality that a foreigner will be hard-pressed to deny is the *ppalli ppalli* ("quickly, quickly") culture of Korea. It's true that Korea, and especially Seoul, has a very fast-paced society. This hurried quality is apparent not only in the fast walking of pedestrians on the street, but also in the speed of public transportation, business transactions, mail, delivery, and even consumption of soju-and-beer bomb shots. It may stem from postwar Korea, when the nation was in a rush to modernize and industrialize. Korea certainly has the results to show for such efforts: in just thirty years, it grew from a third world country to an official developed market, its economy now ranking 13th in the world.

One may notice that Koreans in general are always well-kept and groomed—young people in particular are diligent in keeping up with the latest and hottest trends. In general, Koreans place great emphasis on appearance, as it signifies respect to others (dressing professionally and stylishly for business meetings is absolutely critical). Appearance is also an indication of social and economic success, which, in a country that has developed as rapidly as Korea, can only be regarded as being of great importance.

Q *What is a* jjimjilbang?

I'm still not sure I understand the appeal of *jjimjilbang.* My impression from the first and only time I went was that you basically pay to lie prostrate around a room with other strangers. Honestly, this made me feel more uncomfortable than relaxed. Am I missing something here? What exactly is it that Koreans love so much about *jjimjilbang*?

—Still Stiff

The Korean Dude wonders whether you were able to experience all the different services that *jjimjilbang* have to offer. Aside from the fact that nowhere else in the world allows you to experience this form of sauna-cum-spa, *jjimjilbang* do present many esoteric charms that can be delighted in once you've acquired a taste.

Let's start with a brief introduction. As a rule, all *jjimjilbang* complexes have a *mogyoktang* (bath) section. After a mandatory shower, guests enter this section to get thoroughly scrubbed, using small, rough cloths to rub away dead skin cells. This section also has several soaking tubs, many with natural ingredients like green tea or ginseng.

From here onward, customers don loose-fitting clothing provided at the entrance and settle down for any number of

hours in rooms of varying degrees of heat and humidity. Sauna
rooms are made from different materials, such as yellow earth,
precious stones, and minerals. This is based on the theory that
as you sweat, your body releases toxins and wastes and absorbs
good energy and minerals from each room. It's often an
experience in itself just to explore how many different rooms
one *jjimjilbang* contains.

The *jjimjilbang* is not only a place for health, however.
With the exception of the public baths, the facilities—including
entertainment areas like computer and movie rooms—are
largely coed, so many families and groups of friends come for
some communal R&R.

Korea's love affair with bathing goes back many centuries. Silla, one of the three kingdoms that occupied the Korean Peninsula for much of the first millennium AD, developed a culture of bathing for purposes of ritual purification. Bathing remained important through the subsequent Goryeo (918–1392) and Joseon (1392–1910) eras, when those who could afford it took baths in infusions of ginseng, irises, peach blossoms, or leaves—or even garlic—in order to make their skin whiter. Korea's first modern-style public bathhouse opened in Pyongyang in 1924, during the Japanese colonial period. As modern apartments were built with bathrooms from the 1970s onwards, bathhouses were made partially redundant. At the same time, the bathhouse and sauna came to play a crucial role as social gathering points in an urban environment that lacked other public spaces.

As a segue into his last note, the Korean Dude would like to ask who you went to said *jjimjilbang* with. You may feel more at ease if you partake in the facilities with trusted friends; ultimately, it is the opportunity for socializing in a self-contained, comfortable space, free from outside concerns, that gives *jjimjilbang* their enduring appeal.

GETTING INTO HOT WATER

BY JAMES CREEGAN

It takes a certain amount of bravery to walk into the wet room of a *jjimjilbang* for the first time. Naked but for a locker key around the wrist, clutching a pink scrubbing cloth in your sweaty palm, you might expect a certain amount of staring, pointing, and even gasps. Chances are, however, that fellow users of your local public bath will be far too busy soaking in scalding hot tubs, baking under infrared lights, or scrubbing the city dirt off their skin to care about any new arrivals.

Public baths are an institution in Korea, originating from a time when many people didn't have hot water in their home. They remain popular today as a place to unwind and recharge tired batteries, and can be found throughout the city. Facilities vary according to the size of the building, but even a neighborhood *mogyoktang* (the smallest variety) will have showers, steam rooms, and hot and cold pools—although the facilities may only be for men.

The recent trend, however, is one of larger multi-story complexes called *jjimjilbangs*. Here, bathing is only part of the attraction. A family could easily spend an entire day in the mixed "dry" areas—working out in the gym, getting a massage, eating in the restaurants, reading the comic books, or just taking a nap in the quiet room. T-shirts and shorts are provided, and many places are open 24 hours a day, providing an alternative to hotels or *yeogwans* (small inns) at a rock bottom price.

Bathing areas are (sadly) segregated by sex, and basic etiquette dictates that you shower before using the shared pools. Once cleanliness is taken care of, the key to getting the most out of the experience lies in *yin* and *yang*. For every hot bath you boil in, you should take a heart-stopping dip in the cool pool. And after spending time in a jade-walled steam room, grit your teeth and rinse off with a freezing cold shower.

The idea behind the rapid temperature change is to invigorate the circulation—good for the heart, good for the skin, and nearly unparalleled as a hangover cure. If there are several hot pools, each will have its temperature marked, making it easy to separate the tamer options from the "monkey baths" (where the water is so hot you jump out shouting "Ooh! Ooh! Aah!"). Some of the larger places have taken to scenting the water of a few with lavender or green tea—known as "event baths" (*ibenteu tang*). You may find it useful to ignore the mental image of being simmered in a large stock pot while enjoying the benefits.

The crown jewel of any trip to the *jjimjilbang* is a visit to the only person in the bathing area wearing any underwear. The *ttaemiri* is armed with coarse plastic nets and, for 15,000 won to 30,000 won, gives you an exfoliating treatment to remember as he or she mercilessly scrubs away every square inch of dead skin on your body while you lie on a massage table.

The first time I subjected myself to this startling treatment, I wondered if he was aware that the hair on my chest was actually supposed to be there. When it was all over, not only did I glow as warmly as if I'd spent a day in the sun and had skin softer than peach fuzz, but I also had a pretty good idea of what it would feel like to stumble naked through a car wash.

Female friends of mine swear by this "tough love" beauty treatment and regularly indulge—which leaves me wondering if it wasn't as bad as I remember or gets easier the more times you do it. In fact, if I stay in Korea for another 20 years or so, I may even give it a second try.

2 EDUCATION

Education truly is a first priority for Koreans. People often seek to educate their children even at the price of loneliness and food shortage.

One major factor in this outpouring of energy is Korea's long tradition of respect for scholars. If students are competing to gain precious university entrance spots today with the college entrance examination, it was the national civil service examination, or *gwageo*, that was the focus of education in the past, and the gateway to a career in the government service and the prestige that this entailed. This examination had its origins in the Silla period and rose in importance through the Goryeo period and into the Joseon Dynasty. It was a gateway to the aristocracy for those able to pass the rigorous examination.

The aristocracy may have disappeared, but an elite range of professional positions has risen in its place, and those who hope to move ahead in life gain considerable advantage from an elite education. The vast investment that goes into education is seen by many as the most lucrative down payment on the rewards that later professional employment will bring.

So the fact that early education all but determines the path of an individual for the rest of their life means that many a Korean has a story or a million to relate about bitter memories of childhood. The bulk of these seem to be limited to yawning during constant textbook study, dozing in late-night afterschool *hagwon* (private tutoring company) sessions, and, in the most extreme cases, caffeine overdoses.

This has, of course, had many different results. One is that international comparisons show Korean children to usually excel when compared to other countries. Korea also has an illiteracy rate of less than 2 percent (although some would argue that this is because illiterate individuals go to great lengths to hide their problem). Last but definitely not least, the obsession with education has given birth to a number of unique oddities, including predilections against certain teachers based on race! Let's explore.

Q
What are "wild goose daddies?"

I've noticed that a good deal of my male colleagues here in Korea live alone or with their parents—in fact, many of them tell me that their wives (from whom they are not separated nor divorced) and children are all living abroad in places like the US and Canada, and that they only occasionally see their immediate family during hard-earned work vacations. I couldn't possibly imagine living so far away from my family. Tell me, is there a reason these men do this to themselves?

—Nonmigratory Father

A

What you are witnessing is probably the "wild goose daddy" (called *gireogi appa* in Korean) phenomenon. This phrase refers to the rampant trend of middle-class families whose children and mothers go overseas for education, while the fathers stay behind to work in Korea and support the family, paying occasional visits to the other country. The term likens Korean couples, who remain loyal to each other despite vast distances, to geese, who migrate seasonally and mate for life. Many Korean families choose to send their children overseas, believing either that the Korean education system is too harsh or too competitive for their children, or at times following the children's wish to "go international." Mothers usually move with their children in order to take care of them while they are studying. As a result, there is a significant sadness and loneliness associated with the "wild goose daddy" name.

Other types of "bird daddies" have also emerged in recent years. "Eagle daddies" are those who have the social and economic power and position to visit their family members overseas any time they want. "Penguin daddies" are not technically wealthy enough to educate their children overseas but try their best to support their children's desire to be taught in such a way. Penguin daddies send most of their salary to their children, suffering financial hardship at home in Korea. Poor daddies who cannot send their kids overseas at all are known as "sparrow daddies."

There are many important holidays in Korea, but Lunar New Year and Chuseok are particularly prominent: the former as a day that sets the tone for an entire year's worth of good or bad luck and fortune, and the latter as a day that celebrates the year's harvests. Lunar New Year ("Seol" in Korean) is also the day when all Koreans get a year older (good or bad, depending on your personal approach to maturity).

Both holidays are typically marked as very busy and especially joyous times when families come together to honor ancestors and enjoy one another's company. Here are some more tidbits to help you understand about these special days:

 **Q** *Is the first day of spring fixed in the lunar calendar?*

My Chinese lunar calendar says that the first day of spring is Feb. 4. Is this true for the Korean lunar calendar as well? Also, a Chinese gentleman told me that spring will also commence on Feb. 4 next year, but that doesn't seem to make sense. I know this is a tough question for modern city dwellers, but perhaps an elder from the countryside might know the answer.

—Out from Hibernating

 **A** Yes, the first day of spring, a.k.a. *ipchun*, falls on Feb. 4 on both the solar calendar and lunar calendar. Another yes to the question regarding next year's *ipchun*. Basically, the *ipchun* and the 23 other seasonal subdivisions are based on the movement of the sun, not the moon. But all the subdivisions have gaps from the real weather in Korea, since they were originally made to suit the Beijing area.

Please explain how Koreans advance in age on Chinese New Year regardless of what date they were born on. This doesn't seem right or fair to those who are born in December. For example, if a baby is born on the last day of the final lunar month, it is one year old the next day, and by the following New Year, this baby is legally three years old, even though it's only a year old. How is this correct?

— Age-Phobic

There are various explanations as to the origin of the term Seol (the Korean word for Lunar New Year). One is that it originates from *sal*, which is used as a unit meaning "years" when you count your age. Given the linguistics of this all, it's quite understandable that Koreans might think they gain one *sal* on Seol, even though it doesn't seem entirely correct time-wise. I would refer to this manner as the "traditional" age as opposed to the "real" age. Parents wanted to make their children grow faster by giving them one more year—understandable, given the high infant mortality rate of the past. However, this tradition has now dwindled, since most newborns today are healthy and have long lives ahead of them. Similarly, children are told that they become a year older over a bowl of *tteokguk* (rice cake soup) on Seol. But customs change. Many Koreans today wouldn't agree if you said that you're one year older just because you spent Seol here in Korea.

WELCOMING THE LUNAR NEW YEAR

BY ROBERT KOEHLER

Korea's Seol holiday is rich in tradition, and foreigners need not feel left out. The Lunar New Year ("Seol" in Korean) is one of Korea's two biggest festivals, the other being the autumn harvest celebration, or Chuseok. For Koreans, it's a very busy and especially joyous time when families come together to honor ancestors and enjoy one another's company. For foreigners residing in Korea without family, however, it can be a lonely time accompanied by feelings of accentuated cultural isolation. Let's take a moment to examine Korea's Lunar New Year traditions and the myriad of holiday opportunities open to foreigners so that they might shake the *Seol*-time blues and learn a little about Korea's traditional culture.

Meaning of "Seol"

There are many theories as to what "Seol" means. The first suggests that the word comes from the Korean word *natseolda*, or "unfamiliar." After all, Seol falls on the first day of the new, or "unfamiliar," year. Another theory holds that it comes from *seonda*, or "beginning." How this might tie in to the New Year should be pretty obvious. Furthermore, there are those that say it comes from *seolpda*, an obsolete Korean term meaning "to be careful." Here, the message would be that while you adjust to the new year, you should be careful in your speech and actions.

Tribal Migration

Those new to Korea will no doubt be awed—or horrified—by the traffic conditions that develop as the holiday starts with a major exodus from Korea's major cities. Millions of Koreans hit the roads for their ancestral hometowns in a phenomenon dubbed a "tribal migration" by the local press. This can create some hellacious traffic on outbound lanes at the start of the holiday, and inbound lanes at the end.

Charye

The *charye* is an ancestral ceremony held in the early morning of major holidays, particularly Seol and Chuseok. A table is set with seasonal foods—for example, rice cake soup (*tteokguk*) for the Lunar New Year—and ancestral tablets. Incense is burnt, wine offered to the ancestors, and bows performed. Preparing the food for a *charye*—and the holiday as a whole—can be a grueling task, and women in particular have often found the holiday season to be quite burdensome.

Sebae

After the *charye*, the younger members of the family pay respects to their elders by performing three deep bows. This is called *sebae*. For their troubles, younger performers of the *sebae* will often receive a small gift from their elders—some money, usually. It is traditional to perform these bows in newly made or purchased sets of Korean traditional attire, or *hanbok*. These New Year's Day *hanbok* are called *seolbim*. Neighbors will often visit to pay their respects as well. After the *sebae*, the family will get together to eat the food offered during the *charye*.

Tteokguk

The food most associated with the Lunar New Year is *tteokguk*, or rice cake soup. As the name might imply, the major ingredient of this rich and filling soup is rice cake cut into coin-shaped slices. Prior to slicing, the rice cake comes in a long cylinder, and hence is a symbol of long life. It's said that you grow one year older when you eat a bowl of *tteokguk* on the morning of the Lunar New Year.

Games

A number of folk games, or *minsok nori*, are played on the New Year. The most popular of these is *yut-nori*, a board game (of sorts) played with four sticks that are thrown into the air. As with most games, the rules are a bit difficult to explain and are better learned "hands on." Other holiday pastimes are kite flying, sledding, *tuho* (which involves throwing arrows into a pot), kicking a Korean traditional shuttlecock (called a *jegi*), top spinning, and more. Seoul's royal palaces are especially good places to see these games being played.

Changing Traditions

Korean society has changed dramatically over the last few decades, and those changes have affected the way in which Koreans celebrate the major holidays. For example, more and more of them are using the extended vacation to venture forth to warmer climes such as Southeast Asia or Guam. For many others, however, the holiday is celebrated in much the same way it has been for centuries.

Lonely Foreigners

For foreigners living in Korea, Seol can be a lonely time when the pangs of cultural isolation strike strong. Of course, this is not the case for all foreigners—many are married to Koreans, after all, and are able to enjoy the holidays with their in-laws. Much of Korea shuts down during the extended holiday, so you will find fewer restaurants and shops open, especially on the morning of Seol. That said, a number of locations around Seoul—the royal palaces, Jongmyo, Namsan Hanok Village, and Seoul Museum of History, for starters—have special events prepared during the Lunar New Year holiday to share Korea's holiday traditions with foreigners.

Amusement parks often hold special events and promotions during the holiday as well. The extended holiday also provides an excellent time to travel around and discover Korea, albeit with one caveat—make sure to book train or plane tickets early. Tickets to most destinations around Korea are usually sold out during the holiday, and the last thing you want is to experience Korea's holiday traffic, when a trip to Busan can take up to 15 hours.

One element that cannot be omitted from any description of Lunar New Year is the *jesa*, a ceremony performed by members of a Korean family in memory of deceased ancestors. It is also one of Korea's most important traditional rituals. There is a difference between the *jesa* in general and the aforementioned *charye*, which is what the *jesa* is referred to when it is performed during Chuseok and Lunar New Year's Day. Rites are performed on those holidays as well as on dates throughout the year to mark the deaths of ancestors.

Q *What is a* jesa *like?*

A The two main types of *jesa* are called *gijesa* and *charye*. *Gijesa* are performed every year on the anniversary of an ancestor's death, while *charye* are performed at the traditional festivals of Seol (Lunar New Year) and Chuseok (Harvest Moon Festival).

The *jesa* traditionally takes place after midnight at the home of the eldest son of the eldest surviving generation of the family. A shrine is set up, in front of which a great quantity of carefully prepared cooked food, fruit, vegetables, and rice cakes is laid out. A ritual offering is made to the deceased, followed by bowing. The food from the *jesa* table is then shared among participants. Nearly every family still observes the practice of performing *jesa*, with the exception of Korean Protestants. Korean Catholics do observe the *jesa*.

These days, the *jesa* can be held a tad differently, with some sessions often taking place earlier (between 8 p.m. and 10 p.m.).

Speaking of the deceased, it's also important for any resident of Korea to know what happens in a funeral and what to do as a mourner if the case should arise. As it happens, several people asked the Korean Dude just the right questions about this.

Q *What are Korean funerals like?*

Countries of the world generally seem to demonstrate their own unique character when it comes to funerals. Could you give an overview of Korean funeral traditions?

—Morbidly Curious

A Koreans usually set the mourning period at three days (although this may be extended to five days in very special cases). According to Taoist beliefs, the number one is male and the number two is female, and three is the result of combining one and two, thus indicating "creation."

Mourning usually begins in the home of the deceased or the funerary department of a hospital in a big city or town. Incense and a photographic portrait of the deceased are placed in front of a partition. Relatives and close friends of the family begin to arrive on the first day of mourning to pay their respects after the body has been cleaned, dressed, and placed in a casket. Visitors generally present a white chrysanthemum, light some incense, and bow deeply before the portrait of the deceased. They then bow to the bereaved family, giving either a full bow or a nod.

The practices of burning incense and presenting white chrysanthemums may have originated with efforts to mask the smell of decaying bodies; the flowers came into use at the end of the Joseon Dynasty in the late 19th century. Burning incense is also believed to remove unclean spirits and refresh the body and soul, linking the latter to heaven, and to alert the spirit of the dead. The traditional attire of funerals is white hemp mourning clothing, although black is also a prominent funeral color these days.

On the morning of the last day of mourning, a short ceremony takes place in which eulogies and personal histories of the dead are told, after which the casket is taken for burial.

Some people in rural and agricultural communities still adhere to the practice of carrying the casket all the way to the burial site—although this is becoming extremely rare. Others use a hearse. The burial site is traditionally a spot on a mountainside that has been used by previous generations of the same family, although almost half the dead in Korea are cremated these days.

Interestingly enough, while funeralgoers do mourn, they also have a jolly time with acquaintances, all of them linked together by the departed. Funerals in Korea are traditionally carried out amid a festive atmosphere, since human beings are believed not to die but return to where they originally belonged. Watch director Park Chul-soo's movie *Farewell, My Darling* (*Haksaengbugunsinwi*) for a good picture of how a Korean funeral proceeds. Keep in mind, however, that the movie satirizes Korean society.

 **Q** *Am I supposed to join in Korean funeral services?*

I have been living in Korea for six years, and I would appreciate knowing what to do in the case of the death of a friend or relative. Could you tell us Westerners what we should do if we want to attend a funeral in Korea? For example, if a close friend who is Korean has a relative who passes away, what should we do? Are memorial services normally held in funeral homes in Korea, or are they held at the home of the family? Is it appropriate to arrange to have flowers sent to the family? What do people say when they attend a funeral or memorial service? Would Koreans appreciate a Western friend attending a memorial service, or do they prefer it to be a private, family matter?

—An Uncertain Mourner

 **A** These days, funeral services are usually held at the hospital's funeral center. Most Koreans would welcome and appreciate your visit. When you do go, avoid colorful clothes (although you don't need to strictly follow any funeral dress codes). Prepare an envelope of money for condolences—around 50,000 to 100,000 won.

When you arrive, you'll see a large picture of the deceased up front. You can offer two deep bows and a half bow. If both you and the deceased are Christian, you can say a prayer instead of giving bows after placing your flowers or burning incense (which is usually offered on site). Afterward, you can offer a deep bow to the bereaved family, saying, "I express my deepest condolences." In this case, you can bow your head instead of giving the deep bow. You are then supposed to join the other visitors for food and drinks.

On your way to the dining space, you will find a little desk where you are expected to place your condolence money. You should write your name on the back of the envelope, with word "condolences" on the front. Sending flowers may be a good idea, although some families these days make it clear (usually in the death notice) that they will not accept garlands. This is to avoid unnecessary extravagance (or the appearance thereof). In that case, you can bring a small bouquet of flowers if you'd like. Don't be surprised if the atmosphere in the dining area is unexpectedly jolly; they are expected to foster such a mood for the sake of the bereaved family, especially if the deceased had led a happy life.

At this point, it should be noted that while most funerals are conducted in the manner described above, very different methods are used for traditional Korean funerals, which can still be witnessed on occasion, especially in the countryside. Basically, you should be reserved but not take everything you see too seriously.

THE *JESA* BURDEN FOR KOREAN WOMEN

BY YOUNGHI SEO

During holidays, families gather together and uphold an age-old tradition: the *jesa*, a form of ancestor worship or memorial service for departed family members. Also called the *charye*, this is one of Korea's most important rituals. It gives Koreans an opportunity to reunite, feast, and share the love of culture. It's not without its shortcomings, however—especially for women.

During the *jesa*, an elaborately set table of food is prepared for deceased parents and ancestors. Family members then take turns serving wine and making deep bows to honor the dead. The ritual differs according to family and region. The arrangement of foods is important and often seasonal. During Chuseok, for instance, the table consists of foods from the fall harvest. Fresh fruits like apples, pears, and persimmons are served along with chestnuts and *daechu* (dates). For *banchan* (side dishes), many kinds of autumn vegetables are prepared. Fish, and often meat, is also served, along with soup and grain rice. No *jesa* table is complete without rice cakes—one kind, *songpyeon*, is specially made for the Chuseok holiday.

Interestingly, the *jesa* highlights a significant aspect of Korean society, namely the patriarchal structure of families and deep Confucian roots. It is the duty of the oldest son to organize the ritual and play host to the extended family. Almost all of the legwork falls on his wife. She and the rest of the womenfolk are the ones who stay up all night to prepare the food for the living and dead. During the ritual, only the oldest son and the male line officiate—indicative of society's preference for sons.

Traditionally, women were not allowed to show respect to ancestors through bowing. Instead, they had the honor of serving the men, who feast and drink heartily after the ritual. For women (especially those married to oldest sons), holidays are a stressful time, and the *jesa* is considered an onerous ritual. In fact, oldest or only sons are the least popular choice of mates for Korean women because of the added responsibility of caring for his parents, his immediate and extended family, and the ancestors before them.

Over the years, the *jesa* has been modified into a simpler form in all but the most traditional of families. Some order the food from catering services or buy it ready-made at the market. Due to the stresses of travel and other inconveniences, there are many modern families where only the oldest son and his wife hold the *jesa*, while the others may choose to enjoy the holiday in the city, or even travel overseas. I've heard of families who vote to skip the ritual altogether. But it is ultimately the patriarchs who make the final call.

Rituals are meaningful, and I believe we should try to hold onto them. The act of remembering and honoring our ancestors has value, so a part of me is sad to realize the *jesa* is becoming less and less significant with the passage of time. That's not to say, however, that I think that the burden of preserving the ceremony should fall squarely on the shoulders of the oldest son and his wife. Perhaps it can be shared more equally among all family members, with sons and daughters taking turns organizing and hosting these family reunions.

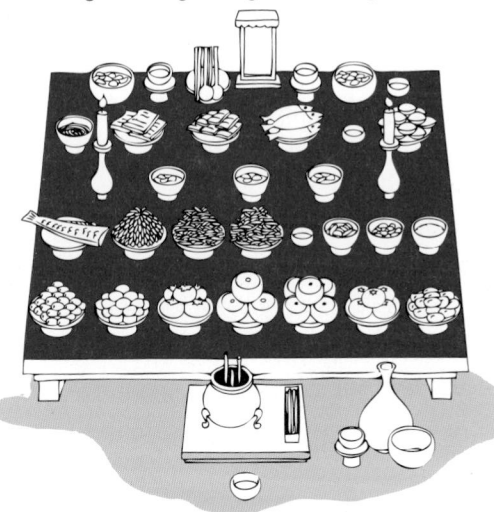

3 WOMEN'S WOES

Korea has made great advances in terms of women's rights and liberties. This is particularly visible in the huge number of women now in the work force. However, longstanding Confucian traditions can be hard to break away from, and Korea may, needless to say, have some way to go yet before it can call itself a truly gender-equal society. For the sake of an honest depiction of Korea, the Korean Dude presents to you—although with no degree of pride—the following concerned inquiries from those who have experienced inequality up close.

 **Are children of single mothers discriminated against?**

A Korean friend and I were recently discussing cultural differences between Canada and Korea and stumbled upon one that I am unable to accept as fact without checking it out. According to her, Korean children born outside of marriage are not able to become full citizens because they cannot receive resident ID numbers. In Korean society, they don't exist. They are unable to go to public school and cannot obtain a license. Is this true? How can this not be seen as a violation of human rights? Is it because of the *hoju* records system?

—Outraged Mother

 Children born out of wedlock are not legally discriminated against. But it is true that they, and their mothers, suffer discrimination and ostracism by society. Indeed, a Korean Women's Development Institute survey found that only about a quarter of Koreans were willing to have an unwed mother as a coworker or neighbor.

It used to be that such children couldn't be registered in the government's *hoju* (family registry) under their mother's name. Indeed, the chauvinistic *hoju* system was long criticized for its refusal to recognize single mothers as family heads.

Fortunately, civil law was finally put in effect in 2008 to get rid of the system.

Things have been improving these days, with the government working to increase payments and add facilities to support and care for unwed mothers. There are also groups dedicated to aiding unwed mothers. AeRanWon is a residential support program for pregnant and parenting women, while the Korean Unwed Mothers Support Network advocates the rights of unwed pregnant women, unwed mothers, and their children.

But Korea still has a long way to go before things really change. In a society that places immense value on bloodlines and social orthodoxy, children of unwed mothers are too often regarded as "unchaste" and "illegitimate," and face great hardships in school life and finding a spouse. Meanwhile, mothers are rejected by society, and even their own families—many are turned out of their home for being "immoral" and treated as near criminals. They often have great difficulty finding jobs and receive very little financial, educational, residential, and medical support from the government. Case in point: the government pays a monthly allowance of 150,000 won per child to adoptive parents, but only 50,000 won for single mothers of dependent children.

This is ironic considering the Korean government constantly frets over the country's birth rate, one of the world's lowest, and deplores Korea's international reputation as an exporter in foreign adoptions. But given the conditions, it is not surprising that so many Korean babies are adopted by overseas parents.

 *What should I do about violence against women in Korea?*

I have been living in Korea for over a year now and am having a wonderful time. But one thing that frustrates me is the violence toward woman and children. I sometimes hear the sounds and cries of women and children being abused by males. I asked my employers what I could do about it, and they told me that it was a Korean woman's responsibility to put up with it. Lame answer. My Korean girlfriend was also punched at a bar by a Korean man while I wasn't there to protect her. When I first came to Korea, I saw a man brutally attack his girlfriend on the street in Insa-dong, in front of dozens of people. No one did anything but avert their eyes as he choked and kicked her to the ground. I was shocked and wanted to help, but felt awkward and held back. I was more culturally sensitive then than I am now. I regret my decision. What would you have done, Korean Dude?

—Protector of Womankind

 The Dude is ashamed to admit that thanks (?) to the influence of Confucian culture, Korea seems to remain one of the least advanced nations in terms of gender equality. According to a 2010 survey, 53.8% answering that they had been victims

of domestic abuse on at least one occasion the year prior. Meanwhile, 39.1 % of them said that they had used corporal punishment on their children during the same period. It turned out that mothers were more likely to spank than fathers.

There have been efforts to improve the situation, including increased media coverage, public awareness campaigns throughout Korea, and the establishment of the Ministry of Gender Equality in 2001. In 1997, the government passed a special act to punish violence against women. It now runs hotlines for female (1366) and underaged (129) victims of violence. These numbers also have English-speaking interpreters available. Many other public and private institutions provide counseling and support for victims, too.

Unfortunately, the law doesn't always function as well as it should in theory. Domestic violence is not an easy problem to solve, partly because it usually takes place in a secluded place (like the home) and is largely considered a personal matter. The cases that you mentioned are also difficult to resolve—even if you call the police, they may arrive well after the assailant escapes. But even if a situation is dangerous, the Dude hopes that Koreans and foreigners alike would show bravery by helping out a person in need and reporting abusers to the appropriate authorities. Taking abuse is absolutely not a woman's responsibility, as your irresponsible employer suggested.

YEONGEO AJUMMA PROVOKES DIVERSE REACTIONS IN HOMOGENEOUS CULTURE

BY ANNE HILTY

Korea has one of the few remaining homogeneous cultures in the developed world: 99 percent ethnic Korean, and a mere 1 percent foreign, with many of the latter group Asian. While many native English speakers have come here to teach, the majority of them in and around Seoul, they still represent a miniscule percentage of the overall population. Once you go outside the greater Seoul area, the foreigners who look distinctly different from Koreans are a true novelty. When my 11-year-old nephew came to visit some years back, he was delighted with all the attention he received. "I'm a celebrity!" he exclaimed, as one Korean after another fawned over him. I told him that they didn't even know his name, and that he was not so much a celebrity as a curiosity. In fact, those who paid tribute to him, saying he was beautiful or touching his head, were simply complimenting me, his presumed mother—which is customary in Korea.

The impact of being a member of a tiny minority in such a homogeneous culture can be quite forceful when you first live here. Seoul initially seemed in many ways like New York, my home—crowded sidewalks and streets and subways, a myriad of sights and sounds, the adrenaline rush that comes from such constant activity and late-night culture. It didn't take long, however, before I became supremely aware of just how often I was the only non-Korean in any given circumstance. Not knowing the language accentuated such differences, though the visual impact was perhaps the greatest acknowledgement of my Otherness.

Dr. Rhi Bou Yong, formerly of Seoul National University and currently the director of the CG Jung Institute of Korea, told me early on that after living in Europe for a number of years, he had concluded that there were four phases to experiencing another culture.

"First, you notice how very different the new culture is from the one you've left behind," he said, "and then you begin to notice all the similarities. Finally, you reach a point where you can comfortably experience both similarities and differences between your culture of origin and the new one in which you're living.

"But," he concluded, "I believe that it's only when you go away and come back again that you can even begin to truly understand this culture that is not your own."

Which is to say, perspective is key. I come from one of the most culturally diverse cities on the planet today: New York. My city was founded by immigrants a few centuries ago, and has never looked back. While this microcosm is surely not without its cultural clashes, it has had enough experience by now to allow representatives from all 192 countries and the dozens of territories and colonies that make up the global community to live in relative harmony with one another. I had had a great deal of interaction with Koreans and other Asians prior to coming here, and the homogeneous nature of Korean culture is one of the primary reasons that I did. I was perhaps less prepared for a monoculture, however, than those who come from less diverse backgrounds.

One of the most obvious barometers for me consists of the reactions that I get from young children, those who are two to four years old by Western calculation. One tiny boy, still preverbal, burst into tears and flatly refused to sit next to me on the subway, despite his mother's urging and murmuring of soothing words. A little girl, perhaps a year older, sought me out in a restaurant in order to snuggle up next to me, practically climbing into my lap. In a museum in Damyang, I heard a father's low chuckles and turned to find his small son following me throughout the museum. Many children point and stare, usually attempting to get a parent or older sibling's attention so that they might identify the stranger in their midst.

I recently got into an elevator with a little boy who was perhaps four years of age. He was with two women who appeared to be his mother and grandmother. When he looked up—and up, and up—to my face, he spontaneously said, "*Yeongeo Ajumma*," looking then to his family for confirmation. When they repeated his words, nodding their heads, he beamed up at me and dubbed me "*Yeongeo Ajumma*" with certainty. I like this reaction best out of all those I've received. To be called an "English-speaking Auntie" by a tiny Korean boy is to be accepted into the society by one of its most innocent members.

1 A TASTE OF HISTORY

By any international standard, Korea is a very modernized society and continues to change rapidly. But signs of its centuries-old traditional culture are still present everywhere in the city. This is hardly surprising, considering that Korea has a 4,300-year-plus history. You will see these elements wherever you go, be they in the form of palaces, monuments, or even the occasional dragon illustration. The stories behind them are fascinating to say the least.

How did Independence Gate survive the Japanese colonial era?

As a longtime expatriate here in Seoul, I am quite aware on the terrible suffering endured by the Korean people and the attempts to destroy all remnants of Korean culture and national identity during the Japanese occupation of 1910 to 1945. That is why I cannot understand why the Japanese would allow the Independence Gate in Seodaemun, which was constructed in 1898, to survive intact. Why was this symbol of Korean freedom and independence tolerated by the Japanese?

—BeMUSED by the Imperials

Let me point out a few more historical facts. It was in 1896 that Koreans broke ground for the Independence Gate—a year after Japan had defeated China in the Sino-Japanese War. Koreans built the gate on the site where Yeongeunmun Gate (built to welcome Chinese envoys) had stood before it was razed. We can assume that the construction of the gate was aimed at China rather than Japan, and that Japan didn't have any reason to oppose it. In fact, the "independence" that the gate refers to is independence from China, a nation to which Korea was virtually a vassal state until Seoul "won" its "independence"

via China's defeat by Japan in 1895. The Independence Club (founded by Seo Jae-pil), which contributed the funds for the gate, included a number of figures who were allegedly close to the Japanese (not entirely surprising, as many reform-minded Koreans at the time were). There are even media reports that the writing on the back of the gate was by Lee Wan-yong, the last prime minister of the Korean Empire, who was made a count by the Japanese for signing the 1910 Treaty of Annexation. Regardless, not only did the Japanese colonial authorities not destroy the gate, they actually helped pay for repairs in 1928, indicating that the Japanese weren't entirely displeased with the structure.

 **Did Koreans burn down Gyeongbokgung Palace?**

On the sign in front of Gyeongbokgung Palace, it says that the Japanese destroyed that palace twice—first during the time of the Hideyoshi invasions, and then again during when Korea was a colony of Japan. But I recently read that Korean folks in the 1590s were so upset that the king and his clan had abandoned the place that citizens themselves burned the place down. Which version is correct?

—Palace Raider

 In a revised version of the *Annals of the Joseon Dynasty* historians corrected their previous position, stating that Gyeongbokgung Palace was burned down by the people, not Hideyoshi's army. After King Seonjo abandoned the capital city in 1592, Gyeongbokgung Palace was set on fire for the first time, since slave (*nobi*) documents were stored in two offices there. The slaves were later joined by Hanyang (today's Seoul) residents, who were infuriated by the fact that the king had left the gates of the city closed. It's quite a shame. In Korea's defense, however, the Korean Dude will let it be said that the invaders were not entirely without blame. This is augmented by the fact that after Japan invaded Korea again in the early 20th century, it installed a massive colonial administration

building (the Joseon Government-General) just behind the Gwanghwamun Gate in an apparent bid to trample Korean pride.

 *Why the dragons in Korean art?*

I'm doing research on the dragon as a motif in culture, mythology, and anthropology. I would like to know something about dragon symbolism in antique Korean art. Could you kindly suggest some bibliographical sources on this topic?

—Cryptozoologically InclineD

 The dragon has probably been one of the most overused animal images since the Three Kingdoms period. Dragon images were used not only in palaces and Buddhist temples but also in personal accessories and handicrafts for the upper class. The dragon was a favored animal of the aristocracy.

In the Joseon era, however, the animal became more public-friendly, as it was first used to decorate white porcelain

for daily use. The once ferocious and dignified beast became very humble and rustic. Some are even described as cute and feeble, like whimpering dogs, while others look like silly old men. If we momentarily ignore the "dragon ball" and the flames spat out by the legendary creature, dragons of the Joseon era sometimes look like unimposing worms and fish. In world art history, dragons have rarely been depicted as humble and easygoing. The Dude actually took this wisdom from a Korean book by Choi Sun-u. Titled *Leaning Against a Pole of the Muryangsujeon* ("무량수전 배흘림기둥에 기대서서"), it was published by Hakgojae in 2002. Another book that you can consult, if you can read Korean, is *Dragon, The Immortal Mythology* ("용, 불멸의 신화"), published by Daewonsa in 1999.

Q *Do people still practice shamanism?*
Can I see a shamanist ceremony?

—Searching for Mudang

Yes, individual shamans do still perform rites—known as *gut*—in Korea today. Many Koreans consult shamans and feel that the rites that they perform are valid and necessary. Some Christians and Buddhists may not regard attending such rites or consulting a shaman to be a bad thing. Although Korean shamanism developed largely in fishing villages and the countryside, shamans also perform rites to address the needs and problems of city dwellers today. Fortune telling is also regarded by some as an aspect of shamanism, and fortune tellers are still widely consulted by Koreans uncertain about the future.

There are several ways to witness shamanistic activity. Some famous *gut* have been designated important intangible treasures and can be seen at festivals around Korea. These include the Namhaean Byeolsin Gut in the province of Gyeongsangnam-do, the Donghaean Byeolsin Gut in Busan, and the Hahoe Byeolsingut Tal-nori in Gyeongsangbuk-do. It is also worth checking out the schedules of traditional performance venues and cultural festivals, as these often feature performances of *gut*. Otherwise, asking around with

Korean friends may well lead you to somebody who knows
when and where to watch a shaman in action. The Korea
Tourism Organization may also be of help; its telephone
number is 1330.

Why red and blue instead of black and white?

Why is the *yin/yang* symbol on the Korean flag blue and red instead of the more familiar black and white?

—WHOLLY INTRIGUED

Yin and *yang* are not most commonly represented by black and white. The two are inseparable from the five elements that the world is believed to be composed of, and each of those elements is associated with a different color: blue, red, white, black, and yellow. They interact on an equal basis rather than being subordinated to one another. Among the colors, blue and red were most frequently used in the daily lives of Koreans, since they were—and to a lesser extent still are—believed to drive out evil forces and bring good fortune. That's why the traditional wedding costume, for example, is blue and red. On the national flag, blue signifies hope, red nobility. In addition, if white and black were used instead of blue and red, the flag would look flat.

Many unique elements of visible (and audible) Korean culture were established more recently, during the latter half of the 20th century, and stemmed from developments such as the Miracle of the Han and, of course, the Korean War. Both monumental events are prime examples of the great tragedies that Koreans have gone through, and the greater resilience born of that.

Q *What's the siren about?*

Recently, I was walking around Apgujeong when I overheard some loud sirens, like a fire drill. Two men were shouting in Korean and pointing at people. I didn't understand what was going on, but it looked serious. I didn't know what was being said. Two days later, it happened again in a different location, Jung-gu, so I know it wasn't an isolated incident. Is there something going on? Should I evacuate the building when I hear this siren?

—Running for Cover

 The siren was for the civil defense drill conducted by the National Emergency Management Agency. When you hear a flat-tone siren, it's a warning. You are supposed to seek shelter in a subway or another safe place. If you are in an office, you are supposed to head down to the basement. When the second siren—a fluctuating tone (for three minutes)–goes off, you are advised not to move in order to avoid unwanted attention from hypothetical enemy planes. The drill started during the Korean War and peaked in the mid-70s, when hostility between South and North Korea reached its apex. Now, the drill has changed into a routine to guarantee public safety in the event of any of the accidents or catastrophes that could happen in a big city. People are growing more and more deaf to the sirens these days, though, so the agency has been experimenting with different kinds of disaster preparedness drills.

 *Colorful roofs in the Korean countryside?*

Whenever I travel through the Korean countryside, I see a lot of orange and blue roofs. Sometimes, it seems like an entire village agreed to have only orange roofs. Is there a special meaning or reason behind these colors?

—Sick of Orange

As part of an effort to modernize Korea, the late President Park Chung-hee introduced the New Village Movement (Saemaeul Undong in Korean) in the 1970s, with the aim of developing agricultural villages. In 1971, some 335 sacks of cement were provided to 33,267 rural towns and used to replace the straw on traditional thatch-roofed houses (*choga-jip*) with roofing tiles. So the tile roofs on most houses were added during nearly the same period. We might surmise, then, that entire villages ended up with new roofs featuring certain designated colors. This government-driven policy was a catastrophe for Korea's rural landscape in the eyes of this Dude, who believes modernization doesn't always mean progress. But what's done is done.

When it comes to colors, we have to take into account the Korean people's color sense when it comes to architecture. Based on the theory of the five elements (*ohaeng*) and *yin/yang*, the traditional Korean *obangsaek* (the five colors of red, blue, yellow, white, and black) have been widely used, with red and blue serving as the main colors. (Think of those Korean temples decorated with splendid primary colors, mostly in red and blue.) Black and white, though widely loved by Koreans since long ago, were not appropriate as colors to promote people's desire to modernize their community. Also, some say that Park may have wanted the roofs to have bright colors in order to make the New Village Movement stand out visually, with a particular emphasis on for the houses located along highways.

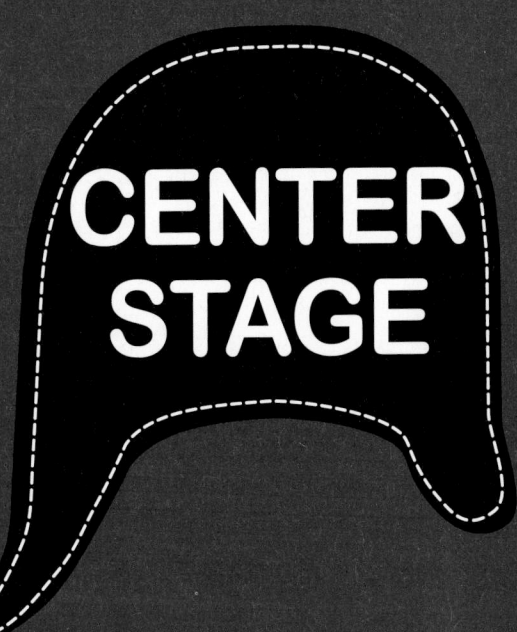

CENTER STAGE

1 MODERN ENTERTAINMENT

Korean nightlife and entertainment have a flavor all their own—not surprising, given that Korea may be one of the most media-centered countries in the world. There is a huge obsession with celebrities and pop culture, and Koreans are constantly updating themselves on current events through light-speed Internet access on their computers, notebooks, and smartphones. Added to this interconnectivity is the community-mindedness of Koreans—many traditional arts are meant to be enjoyed collectively. The marketing of celebrities in acting, dancing, or singing to seem like personal acquaintances rather than untouchable gods seems to be very much related to such concepts.

Appreciation of Korean popular culture has not been limited to natives. In fact, fans all over Asia, and even in the US and Europe, have been going wild for Korean TV series and mainstream music, often referred to as "K-Pop." This has been demonstrated by the popularity of artists such as BoA, Rain, and TVXQ in markets like Japan and China. The likes of Rain and Daniel Henney are even making forays into Hollywood.

Q *What kind of music do young Koreans enjoy?*

I've noticed that K-pop is very popular not just among Korean fans but among people all over Asia, too. Is there a particular taste in or style of music that Koreans gravitate toward and that also appeals to listeners from other completely different cultures? What's going on here?

—Attuned to Pop Culture

A
You could say that young Koreans enjoy a spectrum of music similar to what people enjoy anywhere else in the world. But there are some unique aspects and foci in Korean preferences that form an individual mindset in terms of taste. It does seem that many Koreans tend to favor either mainstream music or more underground indie music—but not both—although tastes have become more international in recent years.

The main type of music enjoyed in Korea is, of course, K-Pop, a catchall term for mainstream music performed by Korean singers. The new K-Pop groups that are currently enjoying the spotlight range from boy bands like Super Junior, Big Bang, Shinee, and 2PM to girl bands Girls' Generation, Brown Eyes, Wonder Girls, and 2NE1, plus old favorites like Lee Hyori. To the foreign ear, many of them seem to have far more appeal as icons and idols than for any particular singing gifts.

Besides mainstream pop, Korea also enjoys thriving hip hop and rock cultures. Hip hop is quite widespread, especially in combination with B-boy culture (see "Why are Koreans so good at breakdancing?" on the next page). The highly acclaimed Drunken Tiger and Epik High have satisfied the domestic hip hop palate, while older and generally very mainstream Jay-Z, Snoop Dogg, and Fatman Scoop tunes comprise the bulk of American hip hop preferences. Meanwhile, rock's broad fan base is evidenced by the Jisan Valley and Incheon Pentaport Rock Festivals. Punk rock—of which bands Crying Nut and Nobrain are major performers—and other indie rock music thrive in the Hongdae area.

The international interests of Korean music lovers are expressed at such multicultural mass events as the Asia Song Festival (which in 2011 featured some of the aforementioned K-Pop artists, as well as Japan's Perfume and AAA, China's

Zhou Bichang, and Hong Kong's Gu Juji). Korea also played host to the Seoul World DJ Festival, an annual international concert and dance event, as well as the 2011 edition of Global Gathering Korea, the world's biggest international dance music festival, featuring world-famous groups Groove Armanda, Digitalism, and Example, alongside Korea's own The Koxx and Ideotape.

Has the Korean Dude been name-dropping here? That's because names and brands (since artists are, ultimately, brands!) are especially valued in Korea. Perhaps the best way to figure out what's really hip in music is simply to visit any café, bar, or other music venue, since you'll hear the most popular recent hits playing over and over and over and over. . . .

 ## *Why are Koreans so good at breakdancing?*

I'm sort of a new fan of breakdancing and was pleasantly surprised to hear that Korea boasts several of the world's top B-boy crews. Only a decade ago, it seemed like Koreans were struggling just to imitate the style at all; now, they're among the forerunners. I was curious to find out if there's a particular reason that Korea thrives in this art form.

—BREAKER

Benson Lee, director of the 2007 film *Planet B-Boy*, once explained, "The powder from hot peppers can be explosive, and so hot that it makes one burn with energy. It's that hot pepper flavor that helps Korean B-boys keep up with the challenges." Are red peppers the sole reason for Korea's success in breakdancing? Perhaps not, but it certainly could be an element!

B-boying remained largely a part of Korean underground culture until the early 90s, when the hip hop/pop group Seotaiji and Boys brought rapping and B-boying to the general public through its songs and music videos. Drawn by the fantastic acrobatics, many young Koreans began trying out B-boying for themselves. Eventually, the collective grew to what it is today, a massively popular culture, although it is still considered to be something of a rebellious movement by more conservative older Koreans.

Most Korean B-boys cite three main reasons for their attraction to breakdancing: a passion for dance, a desire for self-expression that is not readily encouraged by rigid and ascetic Confucianism, and the congenial acceptance demonstrated by the hip hop community. As to why Koreans are exceptionally proficient in it (indeed, Korean B-boys have repeatedly won some of the most prestigious competitions in the world, including Germany's annual Battle of the Year, the Free Style Session in the US, and the traveling Red Ball BC One), elements of B-boying seem to correlate with Korean traditional culture. To illustrate, there seems to be a parallel between the dancing in *nongak*, or traditional farmers' music: both forms appeal to

"commoners" and the public, and are performed in a circle with the dancers in the middle and the audience observing around the action. Both forms also allow and encourage audience feedback and participation.

As beautiful as breakdancing is to watch, there are some very masculine aspects to the art form, with dancers pitting their skills against those of other dancers. This competitive nature, characteristic of Koreans in general, has motivated Korean B-boys to strive to become the best on the international competition scene. It can also be said that the juxtaposition of beauty with masculinity seems to echo the general characteristics of many Korean men, who pay special attention to aesthetics while adhering strongly to their male roles according to Confucianism.

Q

What are some of the most popular non-verbal performances for foreigners?

—ready to go

A

There are a number of modern non-verbal performances that foreigners enjoy.

Nanta and *Ballerina Who Loves a B-Boy* are two performances that have enjoyed wide popularity in Korea and on international stages, including Broadway. *Nanta* is much like *Stomp*: both involve non-traditional dance troupes utilizing unconventional instruments and movements for percussion performances. But *Nanta* relies on kitchen tools like cutting boards and water canisters as instruments, with music based on *samulnori*, a form of traditional Korean percussion music. Meanwhile, *Ballerina Who Loves a B-Boy* is a widely acclaimed breakdancing musical based on the story of a ballerina who falls in love with a B-boy and becomes immersed in the world of hip hop.

Largely based on the traditional movements of taekwondo, the musical *JUMP* also incorporates humor into its performance. It has met with great reviews, earning the top box office award at the Edinburgh Fringe Festival in 2005. Another Festival favorite is *Sa-Choom*, which uses modern dance as its

unique form of expression, blending in everything from hip hop and contemporary dance to breakdancing, tap dancing, and martial arts.

PAN is a traditional performance held at Gwanghwamun Art Hall, a modern theater that was specially opened in May 2008 for *yeonhui*, or traditional Korean performing arts). This genre includes different styles of performing arts such as *buk* (drum) performance, *samulnori* (percussion quartets), *pansori* (narrative songs), masked dance, and *sogonori* (dances with small hand-held drums), all presented in a *madang* (a courtyard space traditionally used for performances).

Finally, *Drawing Show* is one of the world's first attempts at merging art and performance, where performers engulf the viewers in extraordinary onstage live drawing sessions. In addition to painting, the show also incorporates other artistic methods like carving, stamping, rubbing, and marbling, along with entirely new techniques invented by the art director.

As in any other country, television is a hugely popular source of entertainment in Korea, although it seems to have particular prominence here as yet another way to stay connected with Korean popular society. Just from clicking the power button, you may have noticed that there are some unique features to Korean TV. These Westerners offer their observations:

Q What's with the same stars being everywhere on TV?

Watching TV, I have noticed that the same handful of comedians and actresses are everywhere. And, of course, the same ballad singers. It doesn't seem to matter what kind of program or network it is—it's the same people over and over again. I guess they are talented, but having a dinner tray drop on your head or jumping on someone's back doesn't seem to take much talent. Then we see the very same people in TV commercials and print ads and on bus boards, billboards in subway stations, on and on. . . . I have heard many foreigners say the same thing. Korean Dude, what's up with this same, same, same business?

—Star System Boredom

The Korean entertainment industry is driven by the so-called "Star System," a term used in all entertainment sectors, including the film industry, pop music, comedy shows, talk shows, miniseries, and game shows. Networks hire those who appeal to viewers and enjoy wide recognition by the public, thus guaranteeing high ratings. Ironically, these sought-after celebrities and show hosts are in many cases groomed and nurtured by entertainment management companies, though

some did become overnight stars due to their own stellar talent.

It is safe to say that broadcasters and management companies have a symbiotic relationship. The managers try to get promising new faces on TV as often as possible. In theory, the more viewers see them talking, playing games, dancing, singing, and flexing their charms on TV, the sooner the novice will become a star. The more "hot" stars a program has, the higher its ratings. In reality, of course, we often see an obscure talent skyrocket in popularity after appearing on a high-rated sitcom or a particularly memorable talk show episode. But once they become big stars, they disappear from the side shows to be replaced by newer faces.

One development to keep track of is the way powerful entertainer management companies tightly control the entertainment sector of the entire broadcasting industry. In the past, TV program directors (PDs) wielded the power in hiring entertainers, but the tables have now turned. Entertainers got together to form management companies that now hold sway over networks—if a company refuses to send its pool of entertainers, the broadcasters find themselves in a dilemma. To book gifted entertainers, broadcasters must check and double-check schedules in advance—a tedious and troublesome task—so it is more convenient and economical for them to hire several in a "package deal" with a single management company. Management companies will generally send one or two top stars along with several hopefuls—a shrewd business strategy. This saves time and energy for the management companies and broadcasters, but at the expense of variety for the viewers.

Q *Why are products on TV fogged out?*

My Korean partner is a big fan of Korean miniseries, and I have noticed that car and product logos are covered up or "fogged out" on many shots, despite it being very obvious what the products are. Why is this done for some items and not others? Does it have something to do with product placement, which is big business in European TV productions? Or is there some other reason?

—Roland King

A Yes, it definitely has something to do with product placement. But some famous brands get shown because they, said the local advertisement agency official that the Korean Dude interviewed, are so well-known that it's obvious what they are.

Q *Why all the subtitles?*

As a person who is able to function in the Korean language, I find the use of Hangeul subtitles on popular TV shows, especially documentaries or news shows, to be quite strange. I've asked about this with a few native Koreans, and they all tell me that subtitle use is due to the poor sound quality, and that the program wants to enhance what the filmed speaker is saying. Nonsense! In the vast majority of the cases, I can hear what the Korean speaker is saying quite clearly, and the sound quality is fine. While I understand using subtitles when, say, interviewing crime suspects (whose faces are blurred and voices disguised), that reason just doesn't fly when explaining subtitles in documentary programs. You can especially see the excessive use of Hangeul script in the silly Korean comedy shows that pop up to mimic "boing!" noises, the embarrassment of TV stars, and other sounds. Of course, American TV also uses English subtitles, especially during TV news program footage showing illicit sting operations recorded via hidden camera. Still, it seems to me that Koreans use subtitles to a much greater extent than in the West—and unnecessarily so!

—Caption Hater

Formal use of subtitling during news and documentary programs is generally reserved for cases where it is felt that a speaker's comments may not be clearly understood by viewers. Perhaps the speaker is old or speaks with a strong regional accent, or simply too quickly. In this case, the subtitles are an aid to help viewers understand what is being said onscreen.

Over the last decade or so, subtitle usage has expanded, particularly in entertainment programs. It's said that "comic book bubble" subtitles started in Japan, and that Korea followed suit. The biggest side effect of the subtitles is that they intrude on your thinking process—ideas are provided before you can make judgments for yourself. (True, TV is generally that way by nature.) Another is that subtitles promote vulgar slang and incorrect spelling, especially among many younger viewers.

In programs about animals, it's quite common to express the animal's thoughts with subtitles, which is somewhat bizarre. Underlying the practice are commercialism and competition, stirred by the current rating system. Ultimately, though, the audience welcomes it. A college-educated woman in her mid-20s said that subtitles were like having a presenter, and that they sometimes help you catch things that you might otherwise have missed.

 *Any good Korean films?*

What Korean movies would help me understand more about life in Korea?

—Movie Buff

 This is a challenging question even for the Korean Dude! There have been a lot of excellent Korean films with a wide range of themes and styles. They include films on political, social, and historical issues (e.g., *Joint Security Area*), films about pre-modern Korean society (e.g., *Untold Scandal*), and winners at international film festivals (like the now world-famous *Oldboy*).

***Sopyonje* (1993):** Directed by master filmmaker Im Kwon-taek, this was one of Korea's most critically acclaimed films ever both domestically and overseas. The tale of a family of traveling pansori singers, the film sparked renewed interest in Korea's traditional culture.

***Shiri* (1999):** Based on the hunt for a group of elite North Korean spies in South Korea, *Shiri* (directed by Kang Je-gyu; renamed from *Swiri* for its entry into the US) was Korea's first big-budget blockbuster action film.

***Joint Security Area* (2000):** Directed by Park Chan-wook, this film focuses on a tragic friendship between South and North Korean soldiers at the DMZ. Widely praised for its depiction of Korea's national division.

***My Sassy Girl* (2001):** One of the most popular Korean films of all time, this romantic comedy launched the career of one of Korea's most recognized actresses, Gianna Jun. It became mega-blockbuster enough to inspire a terrible American remake starring Jesse Bradford and Elisha Cuthbert, and a Japanese miniseries adaptation with Tsuyoshi Kusanagi and Rena Tanaka.

***Spring, Summer, Fall, Winter...and Spring* (2003):** A beautiful film by notorious art house director Kim Ki-duk that depicts a Buddhist monk through the various seasons of his life. Included by critic Roger Ebert in his list of great movies.

***Oldboy* (2003):** Park Chan-wook's masterpiece, this dark, brutal drama/thriller follows a man seeking vengeance after being imprisoned for 15 years for reasons unclear to him. Quentin Tarantino wanted to give it the top prize at the 2004 Cannes Film Festival.

***Taegeukgi* (2004):** Sure, this film feels a lot like *Saving Private Ryan*, but it's probably the best Korean War film ever made, effectively depicting the brutality of a conflict whose impact is still felt today.

***The King and the Clown* (2005):** Based on a stage play, Lee Jun-ik's film follows two traveling entertainers who are invited into the tyrannical court of Yeonsangun, one of the Joseon era's most notorious kings. It has beautiful depictions of the Korean traditional arts, and its theme of homosexuality at the court proved quite controversial at the time of its release.

***The Host* (2006):** A slick monster flick by director Bong Joon-ho, this film not only spooks but also critically examines Korean society, including the Korea-US relationship and ineffective bureaucracy.

***Secret Sunshine* (2007):** Directed by Lee Chang-dong, this tragic drama—controversial for its criticism of Korean Christianity—won actress Jeon Do-yeon the Best Actress award at the 2007 Cannes Film Festival.

***Old Partner* (2008):** This award-winning indie documentary follows the bond between an elderly farmer and his trusted partner, a 40-year-old ox that he has raised for 30 years, as both face their final days.

***Mother* (2009):** Bong Joon-ho's latest film is the story of Hye-ja, who lives a quiet life with her 27-year-old mentally slow son Do-joon. When he is charged with the murder of a high school student, she strives to prove him, uncovering the dirty secrets of her neighbors along the way.

***Poetry* (2010):** This work by director Lee Chang-dong won the Best Screenplay award at Cannes in the year of its release. Telling the story of a grandmother looking after her sulky grandson and caring professionally for an old stroke victim, *Poetry* involves amateur poetry with several very dark themes and occurrences.

The Crucible (2011): Based on a true and shocking story, via a bestselling book by well-known Korean novelist Gong Ji-young, this movie provoked outrage among local viewers. It tells of the repeated sexual abuse of students by staff at a school for the hearing impaired in southwestern Korea, and of the absurdly light punishments handed out to the perpetrators in court.

The Thieves (2012): The latest film by Choi Dong-hoon, known for his unique crime caper films, *The Thieves* is currently the biggest box office hit in Korean cinema history. It tells the tale of 10 notorious Korean and Chinese thieves who come together to steal a rare diamond from a casino in Macao.

Masquerade (2012): This imaginative historic drama tells the story of the 14th king of the Joseon Dynasty, King Gwanghae (r. 1608–1623). Fearful of assassination and with his court plagued by power struggles and factional strife, Gwanghae finds a strikingly similar-looking comic to play his double. Unlike the violent Gwanghae, the double displays warmth and compassion, which gets the court talking. Eventually, the double begins to make his own voice heard. Actor Lee Byung-hun is especially impressive at switching between the two diametrically opposed characters.

Q *Why is Korea so good at golf?*

—clubber

A Korean golfers, both female and male, have been extremely successful on the world stage in recent years. There are several possible reasons for this. First, many of the successful golfers were born around 1988, and were therefore young enough to be inspired when golfing star Se Ri Pak was becoming globally famous. Koreans love to see compatriots achieving global success, and Pak inspired many young women to take up golf clubs. This ambition combines with the intense training that Korean children tend to devote to becoming the best.

While Koreans feel at a physical disadvantage to people from other parts of the world in other sports, golf relies on accuracy and psychological strength as much as, if not more than, physical power. It may be noted that archery and speed skating are other sports that Koreans excel in at a global level and that involve accuracy and concentration.

Lastly, many traditional Korean "sports" are actually martial arts, in which mental concentration plays a crucial role.

2 TRADITIONAL ENTERTAINMENT

As much of a star as Korea seems to have made of itself on the modern international stage, there are many traditional forms of art and entertainment that prove equally—if not exponentially—more intriguing and intellectually stimulating to aficionados. More good news: viewing and experiencing them has been made relatively easy thanks to national efforts to preserve and practice culture.

 *Who are the Korean geishas?*

With the release of Arthur Golden's *Memoirs of a Geisha*, there was a lot of public interest in traditional, high-class female entertainers. Are there quality books available in English with an informative, insightful, and entertaining (non-academic) account of the *gisaeng*? Also, I understand that geishas still exist and flourish in Japan. Are there still *gisaeng* living and working in Korea? Is there a museum or a place to visit where I can get information on their history and culture?

—Enamored

 As far as this Korean Dude knows, there is no permanent exhibit on *gisaeng*. And while *gisaeng* houses sort of exist today, in the form of *yojeong* (high-class restaurants), it is debatable just how closely these resemble the *gisaeng* houses of old—and what goes on in them is definitely not representative of the *gisaeng* culture that culminated in the Joseon period. However, you can find some accounts of the literary works of *gisaeng* in a book entitled *Fragrance, Elegance, and Virtue—Korean Women in Traditional Arts and Humanities*. Many poems by *gisaeng* are so outstanding and touching that even the Korean Dude knows them by heart.

During the Joseon Dynasty, they were state slave technicians in fields like medicine, stitching, and arts in general. But in the later period of the dynasty, they were divided into three groups; one evolved into authentic government-recognized artists, while another ended up in sex-related industries. In 2006, the MBC network aired a miniseries called *Hwangjini*, based on the story of the titular character, a famous *gisaeng* during the Joseon Dynasty.

Q *What are the representative dance dramas of Korea?*

I've always been enthralled by the kabuki of Japan and the Beijing opera of China, both beautiful and elaborate depictions of the cultural color of their home countries. Now that I'm in Korea, I'm very excited to experience the native theater here. Tell me, what is the Korean equivalent to kabuki or Beijing opera?

—Avid Audience Member

A While kabuki and Beijing opera denote elaborate dance dramas for mostly elite audiences, replete with ornate makeup and costumes, Korean theater was traditionally focused more on performance than on plot and staged for viewing by the general public.

Until the 19th century, the leading forms of Korean public theatre were *talchum*, or "masked dance," and *pansori*, which involves storytelling sessions by a singer and drummer. Neither form had a fixed script—both were handed down orally from generation to generation.

Talchum involved several masked performers who staged dances, dialogue, and song. Concealed behind masks that represented anything from people and animals to supernatural beings, the performers showcased biting satire and parodies that criticized human weaknesses, social evils, and the vices of the privileged class. This had great appeal to audiences—generally commoners—who frequently suffered harsh and severe treatment from the nobility. One notable feature of *talchum* was its encouragement of audience participation—so much so that it was often difficult to distinguish audience member from performer as they all danced together.

Pansori was a popular form of theater during the 19th century. Because of its focus on satire and love stories, and because it encourages audience input (although not quite to the same degree as *talchum*), *pansori* has been compared in impact to the American blues. *Pansori* generally features one *sorikkun* or *kwangdae* (singer), relating stories in rhythm to the beats of a *gosu* (drummer) playing the *buk* (Korean barrel drum). Beats are also given through *chuimsae*, or calls from the audience—similar to the shouts of "¡Olé!" during flamenco performances. *Pansori* comes from the words *pan* (a place where many people gather) and *sori* (sound).

Acknowledgement

Most of the questions and answers in this book are from *SEOUL* magazine, which I began as a guide for foreigners curious about Korea and her culture. When I began publishing the monthly magazine in 2003, I had no idea it would take up so much of my life. Accordingly, my first thanks go out to my family for their tolerance and patience for all the hours I needed to spend at the office. I also thank the writers and editors of *SEOUL*, without whom this book would not have been possible. In particular, special thanks go to Alex Kim, copy editor for *SEOUL* in 2004, for coming up with the creative name for the column from which this book takes its title. Special thanks should also be extended to Robert Koehler, chief editor of *SEOUL*, copy editor, Colin A. Mouat, and reporters Choi Misun and Ryu Youngmi for sometimes writing and editing answers when the Korean Dude was otherwise indisposed. For the book's overall content, I am greatly indebted to Irene Park, book editor at Seoul Selection, who framed the structure of the book, editing the Dude's otherwise awkward explanations and often adding her own opinions as a Korean-American Dudette. A debt of gratitude also goes to *SEOUL*'s readers, who submitted many of the questions found in this book. The eye-catching layout and eloquent illustrations are thanks to graphic designers Lee Bok-hyun and Kim Hyun-ji. Last but not least, thanks goes to Park Hye-young for beautifully wrapping up this work as book editor.

Kim Hyung-geun
Samcheong-dong, Seoul, Korea
Spring, 2012

CREDITS

Writer   Kim Hyung-geun (Hank Kim)
Contributors   Jisu Ahn, Joel Browning, James Creegan, Kelli Donigan, Scott Fallis,
Richard Harris, Anne Hilty, David Kendall, June Kim, Nancy Kim,
Robert Koehler, Younghi Seo, Elizabeth Shim, Richard Stansfield,
Andrew Petty, and Joanne Yun
Publisher   Kim Hyung-geun
Editors   Irene Park, Park Hye-young
Copy Editor   Colin A. Mouat
Designers   Kim Hyun-ji, Lee Bok-hyun